Picnics, Potlucks, & Porch Parties

Picnics, Potlucks, & Porch Parties

Recipes, Menus, and Ideas for Every Occasion

AIMEE BROUSSARD

QUAIL RIDGE PRESS

Preserving America's Food Heritage

To Brian,
Husband, Soulmate, Taste Tester,
Personal Dishwasher, Camera Holder,
and Best Friend. Of your many titles,
Head Cheerleader
is the one I'm most grateful for.
I am who I am because of you.

Library of Congress Cataloging-in-Publication Data

Names: Broussard, Aimee, author.
Title: Picnics, potlucks, & porch parties : recipes & ideas for every
    occasion / by Aimee Broussard.
Other titles: Picnics, potlucks, and porch parties
Description: Brandon, MS : Quail Ridge Press, [2015] | Includes index. |
    "Preserving America's food heritage."
Identifiers: LCCN 2015041646 | ISBN 9781938879166 (pbk.)
Subjects: LCSH: Entertaining. | LCGFT: Cookbooks.
Classification: LCC TX731 .B756 2015 | DDC 642/.4--dc23
LC record available at http://lccn.loc.gov/2015041646

ISBN 978-1-938879-16-6

Manufactured in the United States of America
First edition, May 2016

QUAIL RIDGE PRESS
P. O. Box 123 • Brandon, MS 39043 • 1-800-343-1583
info@quailridge.com • www.quailridge.com

Contents

Preface

"Sometimes you find yourself in the middle of nowhere; and sometimes, in the middle of nowhere, you find yourself." –Unknown

I grew up idolizing my grandmothers. My Grandma Eloise was daring, assertive, and smart. I was so impressed that she boarded a train to Nashville by herself back in the 1930s to earn a graduate degree! My creative Little Maw Maw, named after her petite size, was always teaching me—putting me in summer camp sewing classes, attempting to teach me to paint, and always encouraging me to make handmade gifts. I learned a lot from them.

After graduating from college, I landed a great job, and a few years later married the love of my life in a gorgeous plantation setting that I had dreamt of since childhood. My career ambitions didn't seem so wonderful when they required me, at a moment's notice, to travel sometimes 3,500 miles away, saying goodbye to my new home and new husband. It wasn't long before I bravely decided to *quit!* Now, bidding farewell to my former self, I would get to—no, *have* to—call on my creative side. I had lots of support...and faith.

With all the newly found free time on my hands, rather than being idle, or looking for another job that didn't require travel, I took the initiative—with encouragement from my mother—to teach myself to sew and cook. I savored this time and endeavored to make every single one of my husband's family's favorite recipes out of the recipe box my sister-in-law, Ricci, gave me at one of my wedding showers. As a new wife, I wanted to create them all for him. And I did!

As I was cooking and sewing my days away, I entered a contest for a chance to win a trip to New York City and a wardrobe makeover with fashion guru, Tim Gunn...and I won! The clothes I received were wonderful, but the highlight was explaining to Mr. Gunn how to construct a famed New Orleans Doberge Cake! It was during this experience that I began a blog, to invite friends and family to share my experiences, and to virtually join me on my adventures.

If that wasn't enough excitement, I managed to land back in NYC, this time at the Martha Stewart headquarters, surrounded by eighty female business owners who were turning dreams into action plans. The event, called "Dreamers into Doers," was a trip that would further define my realization that following your heart and doing what it is you truly enjoy is the *real* definition of success.

I continued to add to my blog, all the while challenging myself to learn new skills, such as food styling and photography. I also opened an online shop of handmade aprons. I was becoming quite creative with recipes, too. My Pecan Praline King Cake Cookies took home top honors during a food blogging bake-off in Virginia. True to my bayou belle ways, the cookies were Mardi Gras colors of green, purple, and gold, and decorated with Mardi Gras beads all around. And I won again! Talk about a boost of confidence! This gave me added determination to keep moving forward.

At this point, I had plenty of fun stories, photos, and recipes for my fast-growing blog, but what was and continues to be just as important as sharing my stories, is connecting with my readers, and learning more about *their* stories, and the food that fills their hearts and homes.

Fast forward to my latest endeavor, where I create and share an entire cookbook of easy recipes and ideas for fun outdoor entertaining. You are holding it! Inside this book, you'll find, not only some of my family favorite recipes, but also popular recipes from my blog, as well as tips and tricks to become an overnight hostess success with minimal effort. A quick trip to the craft store for a few happies, and a bundle of grocery store flowers can add new life to your outdoor entertaining preparations. It doesn't have to be fancy or costly; it only matters *how special and welcome you make your guests feel*.

Whether you're heading to a potluck dinner and need a side dish, coordinating an impromptu afternoon picnic with someone special, or decking out your front porch for a neighborhood celebration, you'll find inspiration, helpful hospitality suggestions, and oodles of easy, delicious recipes right here! Life is oh so much better when sharing a meal together, and I cordially invite you to share one with me. I'll have your lemonade ready and your porch cushions fluffed!

Aimee Broussard
(aimeebroussard.com)

Party & Menu Plans

Country Cozy Fried Chicken Picnic

Lovely Little Lunch on the Porch

Muffins for Moms Recipe Exchange

Backyard BBQ Family Reunion

Easter Bunny Brunch

Patriotic Porch Party

Neighborhood Potluck Gathering

It's Tailgate Time!

Friendsgiving Feast

Home for the Holidays

Beverages

Beverage Labels

Long gone are the days of boring paper food tents. Inexpensive wood cutouts from the craft store become beverage label sensations with a little bit of wood stain or paint, lettering, and twine.

Almond Tea

SERVES 8 OR MORE

8 cups cold water, divided

9 tea bags

1 cup sugar

1 teaspoon vanilla extract

1½ teaspoons almond extract

Juice of 3 lemons

1) In a saucepan, bring 2 cups water to a gentle boil. Add tea bags; cover, and remove pan from heat. Steep 10 minutes.

2) Remove tea bags, but don't squeeze them. Pour tea into heat-resistant 2-quart pitcher; add sugar; stir until dissolved.

3) Stir in vanilla, almond extract, lemon juice, and remaining 6 cups water. Cool, then refrigerate. Serve in glasses over ice.

Amaretto Slush Punch

MAKES 1 GALLON

Perfect for a summer evening on the porch when you'd like something cool and refreshing.

1 cup sugar

1 cup plus 6 ounces water, divided

1 (2-liter) bottle Sprite

1 (6-ounce) can frozen orange juice concentrate

1 (28-ounce) can pineapple juice

1 cup amaretto

1 (4½-ounce) jar cherries, undrained

1) Make a simple syrup by bringing sugar and 1 cup water to a boil.

2) Mix Sprite, orange juice concentrate, pineapple juice, and remaining 6 ounces water in large container. Stir in simple syrup, amaretto, and cherries.

3) Freeze (can use gallon zip-close bag). Take out 1–2 hours prior to serving, so it is "slushy."

Tipsy Peach Tea

SERVES 8

3 large tea bags for iced tea

3 cups boiling water

8 fresh mint sprigs

4 cups lemonade, made from frozen concentrate

½ cup vodka

1 lemon, sliced for garnish

1 peach, sliced for garnish

1) Let tea bags steep in 3 cups boiling water for 5–7 minutes. Carefully discard tea bags, and let tea cool.

2) Place mint sprigs in a large pitcher; mash with a muddler or handle of a wooden spoon until slightly bruised. Pour in tea, lemonade, and vodka. Chill in refrigerator before serving.

3) Fill 8 highball glasses or Mason jars with ice. Pour tea among glasses. Garnish with lemon and peach slices.

Café au Lait Punch

SERVES 20 OR MORE

My great-grandmother Thibodeaux taught me what café au lait meant (French for coffee with milk), and even allowed me to indulge in it when visiting her home as a young lady. I felt oh so very grown up sipping what I believed was reserved for adults only. Imagine my delight when experiencing my beloved café au lait blended with ice cream! This punch is the perfect treat for summer porch sipping when the temperatures begin to rise.

2 ounces instant coffee

2 cups sugar

1 cup water

1 gallon whole milk (no substitutes)

½ gallon vanilla ice cream

½ gallon chocolate ice cream

1) In saucepan, mix coffee, sugar, and water; heat until sugar dissolves. Refrigerate. Liquid will get syrupy.

2) Before guests arrive, pour chilled syrup into punch bowl. Add entire gallon of milk, and stir to combine.

3) Scoop all ice cream into punch; stir. The ice cream doesn't have to melt all the way—it will keep the punch cold.

Tip: Coffee punch, while delicious, can look a little boring. Place whipped cream and cinnamon sticks on your serving cart and allow your guests to fancy things up a bit.

Peach Cobbler Wobbler

SERVES 10 OR MORE

64 ounces white grape-peach juice

1 cup brown sugar

4 ripe peaches, peeled and quartered

3 whole cinnamon sticks

¾–1½ cups Everclear (to your taste)

½ cup peach schnapps

Mint sprig for garnish

1) Add juice, brown sugar, peaches, and cinnamon sticks to a large pot. Bring to a low boil for 3–4 minutes, or until sugar dissolves. Cool to room temperature.

2) Stir in Everclear and peach schnapps. If you're serving within 24 hours, pour into an airtight container, and refrigerate.

3) If serving in a couple of days, strain peaches (reserve peaches for a cobbler). Refrigerate liquid in airtight container.

4) Serve over ice with a sprig of mint.

Cran-Orange Mimosas

SERVES 12

4 cups cranberry juice, chilled

4 cups orange juice, chilled

2 (750-ml) bottles champagne, chilled

12 orange slices for garnish

Frosted Cranberries for garnish (page 25)

1) Fill 12 (12-ounce) glasses with ice; pour ⅓ cup cranberry juice into each glass. Top each serving with ⅓ cup orange juice, and about ½ cup champagne.

2) Garnish with an orange slice and a cocktail pick with Frosted Cranberries.

Southern Sweet Lemonade
with Strawberries

Southern Sweet Lemonade

MAKES 1½–2½ QUARTS

There are few things sweeter than a glass of homemade lemonade, and a picnic just isn't quite complete without its presence. With a variety of ways to jazz up this sweet and delicious beverage, it remains at the top of my picnic planning agenda.

1 cup sugar

1 cup water (for simple syrup)

1 cup fresh lemon juice (4–6 lemons)

3–4 cups cold water

1) Make a simple syrup by heating sugar and 1 cup water in a small saucepan until sugar dissolves completely.

2) While sugar is dissolving, juice lemons.

3) Add lemon juice and simple syrup to a pitcher. Add 3–4 cups cold water, more or less, to desired strength. Refrigerate 30–40 minutes. Too sweet? Add more lemon juice. Not sweet enough? Add more cold water.

NOTE: For more intense lemon flavor and stronger color, zest 1 fresh lemon, and add to simple syrup as you are making it. Once sugar has dissolved in the water, remove from heat, and let zest steep several minutes, then strain when you add the simple syrup to the lemon juice.

Make Mine Strawberry!

Purée 1 pint of strawberries in a blender with ½ cup water. Strain, if desired; add to lemonade. Garnish with lemon and a sliced strawberry.

Make Mine a Cocktail!

In an 8-ounce Mason jar, muddle 3 basil leaves, and fill with ice. Add 1 ounce gin and 2 ounces strawberry lemonade to a shaker, and fill with fresh ice. Shake, and strain into prepared Mason jar. Top with a splash of club soda, and garnish with a strawberry and a basil leaf, if desired.

Bunny Tail Peach Bellinis

SERVES 3 OR 4

2½ ounces peach schnapps

4 ounces champagne

1½ ounces vodka

8 ounces frozen sliced peaches

1 cup ice

1) In a blender, combine peach schnapps, champagne, and vodka.

2) Drop frozen peaches into blender with ice. Close lid, and blend on high for about 30 seconds, or until smooth. Pour into 3 or 4 tall glasses.

Bellini Cottontails

Easily create bunny "tails" for your Bellinis by adding white pom poms or cotton balls to the bottom of the glasses with a bit of hot glue. Don't worry about ruining your glasses; the hot glue isn't permanent, and will easily peel off at the end of the day. Cutely decorated beverages aren't just for kids!

Red, White, & Blueberry Sangria

SERVES 8–10

1 bottle dry white wine

1 cup white grape juice

2 cups fresh blueberries

1 pound fresh strawberries, hulled and sliced

1 (750-ml) bottle champagne

3–4 Granny Smith apples, thinly sliced (may substitute pears or pineapple)

1) Stir together white wine, grape juice, blueberries, and strawberries in a large pitcher. Cover, and refrigerate 1–4 hours, so flavors can meld. (The longer the mixture sits, the more red it will become.)

2) When ready to serve, stir in champagne, apples, and ice. Serve immediately.

Fun Idea: Cut apple slices with a star-shaped cookie cutter; iimmediately add to sangria to prevent browning.

Ponchatoula Punch Cocktails

SERVES 4

3 tablespons sugar

1½ ounces water

4 (2-inch) sprigs fresh thyme

8 ounces sliced stemmed strawberries

3 ounces gin

1½ ounces crème de cacao

1½ ounces blood orange liqueur

3 ounces fresh lemon juice

1) Heat sugar and water in saucepan until sugar dissolves. Cool.

2) In a large pitcher, muddle fresh thyme and strawberries. Add all liquid ingredients, and stir well.

3) Double strain into cocktail glasses. Garnish each glass with a slice of strawberry and an extra sprig of thyme.

Early Kickoff Bloody Marys

SERVES 6

2 cups vegetable juice cocktail

1½ cups vodka

1 cup cocktail sauce

Juice of ½ large lemon

Juice of 1 small lime

2 teaspoons cracked black pepper

1 teaspoon Tabasco

Dash of cumin

Celery salt to taste

6 celery stalks (inner stalks)

12 pickled okra pods

12 spicy pickled green beans

1) Combine vegetable juice cocktail, vodka, cocktail sauce, lemon and lime juice, black pepper, Tabasco, and cumin in a large container, and mix well.

2) Moisten rims of 6 glasses with water, and rotate the rims in celery salt to cover evenly. Fill glasses with ice, and strain Bloody Mary mixture into glasses.

3) Serve with celery stalks, pickled okra, and pickled green beans.

Christmas Cosmos with Frosted Cranberries

SERVES 1

1½ ounces vodka

½ ounce triple sec

1 ounce cranberry juice

Rosemary sprig for garnish

FROSTED CRANBERRIES:

2 cups sugar, divided

½ cup water

1 (12-ounce) bag fresh cranberries

Shake vodka, triple sec, and cranberry juice with ice in a cocktail shaker. Strain into a martini glass.

1) Garnish with a sprig of rosemary, and a couple of Frosted Cranberries.

2) **Frosted Cranberries:** Mix ½ cup sugar and ½ cup water in a medium saucepan over medium heat until sugar is dissolved.

3) Stir in cranberries until well coated. Using a slotted spoon, transfer to a mesh rack; let dry at least an hour.

4) Working in batches, roll dry cranberries in remaining 1½ cups sugar until well coated. Let dry for another hour.

Appetizers

Mason Jar Grab & Go

Mason jars and outdoor entertaining go together like peanut butter and jelly. There are so many different ways to utilize them in your party-perfect plans: for food storage, for serving individual portions, or for neatly organizing the day's necessities. I call these "grab and go" because you *grab* your drinking glass, a themed straw, your utensils, a handkerchief napkin, and well, you *go* enjoy your meal!

BBQ Deviled Eggs

BBQ Deviled Eggs

MAKES 1 DOZEN

My husband calls me the "Queen of Deviled Eggs," but, like for my lemonade, I just get so gosh darn excited about all the varieties you can come up with to enhance America's most beloved appetizer. These BBQ deviled eggs even promote healthy marriages. How, you say? Just add your significant other's BBQ to your deviled egg recipe, and just you wait and see if they don't win the highest rating for the most favorite eggs to date!

6 large hard-boiled eggs, peeled

¼ cup mayonnaise

1½ tablespoons sweet relish

1 tablespoon Dijon mustard

1 cup finely chopped Classic BBQ Chicken (page 47)

Salt and black pepper to taste

2½ tablespoons barbecue rub

2 tablespoon chopped green onions

1) Halve eggs lengthwise. Remove yolks, and place in a small bowl; mash with a fork. Stir in mayonnaise, relish, Dijon mustard, chicken, salt, and black pepper. Mix well.

2) Spoon mixture back into egg white cavities, or use a piping bag to pipe more neatly. Lightly sprinkle with BBQ rub, and top with green onions.

3) Serve immediately, or cover and refrigerate for up to 4 hours, until ready to serve.

No-Fail Hard-Boiled Eggs

Place uncooked eggs in a saucepan, and add enough cold water to completely cover eggs. Do not overcrowd eggs. Add 1 tablespoon salt, and heat on high until it reaches a boil. Remove from heat, cover, and let sit 12–15 minutes. Drain, and place eggs in a bowl of ice water for easy peeling.

Honey Garlic Party Meatballs

MAKES ABOUT 5 DOZEN

When the Taste of Home Cooking School asked me to create a signature dish using pork, I thought to myself, why not use pork rather than beef in a delicious meatball? A "fancy" meatball to serve at gatherings when you want to impress your friends...a meatball that is far from merely being just an ordinary meatball. And hence, the Honey Garlic Party Meatballs were born. I call them "Party" because they were prepared on the Taste of Home Cooking School stage in numerous locations, across four states, and "partied" as hard as any meatballs ever could.

MEATBALLS:

2 pounds ground pork

¾ cup bread crumbs

1 egg

½ teaspoon salt

¼ teaspoon black pepper

1 clove garlic, pressed

SAUCE:

2 teaspoons melted butter

2 medium garlic cloves, minced

½ cup ketchup

¼ cup honey

1½ tablespoons soy sauce

2 teaspoons Tabasco

1) Combine all Meatballs ingredients, and form into 1- to 1½-inch round balls. Brown in a large skillet over medium-high heat; turn heat off, and drain.

2) In a separate bowl, whisk together Sauce ingredients.

3) Pour Sauce over Meatballs, and simmer, covered, 30 minutes. Serve warm.

Brown Sugar Smokies

SERVES 6

1 pound cold bacon, strips cut in thirds

1 (14-ounce) package smoked cocktail sausages

1 cup packed brown sugar

1) Preheat oven to 350°. Line a large rimmed baking sheet with aluminum foil.

2) Wrap a bacon piece around each sausage, securing with toothpick. Arrange on a baking sheet and sprinkle with brown sugar, pressing sugar onto sausages.

3) Bake 30 minutes, then flip sausages, and broil until bacon is crisp, and sugar is melted, 1–2 minutes. Cool slightly.

Potato Rounds

MAKES 24 ROUNDS

2 large unpeeled baking potatoes

Vegetable oil

1 cup shredded Colby Jack cheese

6 bacon slices, crisply cooked, drained, crumbled

⅓ cup sliced green onions

¼ cup barbecue sauce

1) Preheat oven to 450°. Using a mandolin, slice potatoes into ¼-inch slices.

2) Generously brush vegetable oil on both sides of slices. Place on a baking stone or pan, and bake 20 minutes, or until lightly browned; remove from oven.

3) Combine cheese, bacon, and green onions in a medium bowl. Spoon barbecue sauce onto each potato slice, sprinkle with cheese mixture, and return to oven. Bake 3–5 minutes, or until cheese is melted.

Marinated Tomato Rounds

SERVES 8–10

Easy and delicious, these are great served in the summertime when tomatoes are in season and when everyone is trying to wiggle into a bathing suit.

8 tomatoes, thickly sliced

2 tablespoons balsamic vinegar

2 cups fresh spinach

1 tablespoon minced garlic

1 tablespoon lemon juice

Salt and black pepper to taste

½ cup shredded Italian cheese blend

1) Marinate tomatoes in balsamic vinegar for 4–6 hours. Place in a baking pan, and bake at 350° for 7 minutes, or until slightly tender.

2) Sauté spinach and garlic until wilted; add lemon juice, salt, and black pepper.

3) Set oven to broil. Place tomatoes on nonstick foil-lined baking pans. Spoon spinach mixture onto tomatoes, and sprinkle with cheese. Broil just until cheese is golden.

Fruit Kabobs with Lemon Yogurt Dip

SERVES 6–10

1½ cups lemon yogurt

1½ cups whipped topping

2 teaspoons honey

1 teaspoon vanilla extract

½ watermelon, seeded, balled

1 cantaloupe, balled

1 bunch grapes

1 pineapple, cut into chunks

1) Combine yogurt, whipped topping, honey, and vanilla. Refrigerate until ready to serve.

2) Skewer the fruit, alternately on wooden skewers. Serve with the yogurt dip.

Marinated Shrimp in Mustard Sauce

SERVES 8–10

Also really good in a shrimp salad!

¼ cup tarragon-flavored vinegar

¼ cup red wine vinegar

1 cup prepared mustard

1 teaspoon black pepper

2 teaspoons red pepper flakes

2 teaspoons salt

½ cup vegetable oil

¼ cup flat leaf parsley, minced

6 green onions, chopped

3 ounces crab and shrimp boil

2 pounds uncooked medium shrimp, peeled, deveined

Cucumber slices

Crackers

1) In a bowl, whisk together vinegars, mustard, black pepper, pepper flakes, and salt. Slowly whisk in oil until slightly thickened. Stir in parsley and green onions; set aside.

2) Fill 6-quart pot half full of water; add crab and shrimp boil. Bring to a boil, simmer 3–4 minutes. Add shrimp to hot water; cook just until pink, 2–3 minutes.

3) Quickly pour shrimp into a colander; shake to remove excess water. Stir drained shrimp into mustard sauce. Cover, and refrigerate overnight, or up to 2 days.

4) To serve, spoon into a serving bowl. Serve with cucumber slices and crackers.

Pimento Cheese Poppers

SERVES 24

Pimento cheese is delicious in so many ways…served like this, or with crackers, on finger sandwiches, or stuffed in a burger (see below).

PIMENTO CHEESE:

1 large pimento or sweet red bell pepper, halved

Olive oil

Sea salt to taste

1 pound sharp white Cheddar cheese, shredded

4 tablespoons mayonnaise

¼ cup minced red onion

½ teaspoon garlic

½ teaspoon black pepper

Salt to taste

POPPERS:

24 tricolor sweet mini peppers, halved lengthwise, seeded

2 cups Pimento Cheese

Freshly ground black pepper (optional)

1) **Pimento Cheese:** Preheat oven to 450°. Place pepper halves on baking sheet, brush with olive oil, and sprinkle with salt. Roast until skin is blistered, about 15 minutes. When cool enough to handle, remove the peels, chop, and place in a large bowl.

2) Add cheese, mayonnaise, red onion, garlic, and black pepper. Gently stir until pimentos are evenly mixed, and mayonnaise binds with cheese. Add salt.

3) **Poppers:** Stuff each pepper half with about 2 teaspoons Pimento Cheese. Sprinkle with black pepper, if desired. Refrigerate until ready to serve.

Pimento Cheese-Stuffed Burger

Spoon 1½ tablespoons Pimento Cheese in center of a 4-inch hamburger patty. Top with another hamburger patty, pressing edges to seal. Sprinkle with salt. Cover, and chill at least 30 minutes. Preheat grill to 350°–400°. Grill burgers with lid closed 7–8 minutes on each side, or until beef is no longer pink. Serve on buns with desired toppings.

Twisty Pretzels with Beer Cheese Dip

MAKES 1 DOZEN

1 (0.25-ounce) packet active dry yeast

2 tablespoons packed brown sugar

1⅛ teaspoons salt

1½ cups warm water

3 cups all-purpose flour

1 cup bread flour

2 cups hot water, divided

2 tablespoons baking soda

1½ tablespoons butter, melted

2 tablespoons coarse kosher salt

CHEESE DIP:

1 (12-ounce) bottle beer

3 cups grated Cheddar cheese

2 tablespoons flour

1 (8-ounce) package cream cheese, cubed and softened

1 clove garlic, minced

Salt and black pepper to taste

1) Dissolve yeast, brown sugar, and salt in warm water in a large bowl until foamy.

2) Stir in both flours. Turn dough onto floured surface; knead until smooth and elastic, about 8 minutes. Place in greased bowl, turning to coat. Cover, and let rise until double in size, about 1 hour.

3) Preheat oven to 450°. Line 2 large baking sheets with parchment paper. Combine 2 cups hot water with baking soda in a shallow bowl or pan.

4) Turn dough onto floured surface, and cut into 12 equal pieces. Roll each into a thin rope, and twist into pretzel shape. Dip each into baking soda mixture. Transfer to baking sheets, 6 per sheet, 2 inches apart.

5) Bake 8–10 minutes, turning halfway through. Brush pretzels with melted butter, and sprinkle with kosher salt. Transfer to a wire rack to cool.

6) **Cheese Dip:** In a saucepan over medium heat, bring beer to a simmer. In a bowl, toss cheese with flour. Add cheese mixture to beer with remaining ingredients. Stir until cheese has melted, and texture is smooth, about 5 minutes. Strain through a fine mesh strainer. Keep warm until ready to serve.

French Bread Crab Dip

French Bread Crab Dip

SERVES 8–10

Anytime we have friends over for a football watching party (we call it "homegating" when your team is on the road and you can't tailgate), my husband says, "Let me guess—you're making the crab dip." But I can't help it; it's the perfect dip to serve when hosting friends. It's even great baked on its own, without the French bread loaf, and served with crackers.

3 cups shredded sharp Cheddar cheese

1 pound lump crabmeat, free of shells

¼ cup finely chopped onion

¼ cup finely chopped green onions

½ cup mayonnaise

1 (8-ounce) package cream cheese, softened

1 teaspoon Worcestershire

Salt and black pepper to taste

1 loaf French bread

1) Mix cheese and crabmeat together. Add onion, green onions, mayonnaise, cream cheese, Worcestershire, salt, and black pepper. Refrigerate in an airtight container for several hours.

2) Preheat oven to 350°.

3) Cut top off bread, and hollow out. Save bread pieces for dipping.

4) Spoon the dip into hollowed-out bread loaf, and bake 35–40 minutes. Use reserved bread pieces and crackers for dipping.

Game Day Muffuletta Dip

MAKES 4 CUPS

If you've never had a New Orleans muffuletta, it's basically a sandwich piled high with salami, ham or other deli meats, and cheese, topped off with a zesty olive salad on seeded round Italian bread. They are gigantic, delicious, and can be a bit messy. This dip embodies all the flavors of the sandwich in an easy-to-eat and easy-to-transport dip.

1 cup Italian olive salad, drained

1 cup diced salami (about 4 ounces)

¼ cup grated Parmesan cheese

¼ cup chopped pepperoncini salad peppers

1 (2¼-ounce) can sliced black olives, drained

4 ounces provolone cheese, diced

1 celery stalk, finely chopped

½ red bell pepper, chopped

1 tablespoon olive oil

¼ cup chopped fresh parsley

French bread crostini

1) Stir together all ingredients except parsley and crostini. Cover, and chill 1 hour, or up to 24 hours, before serving.

2) Stir in parsley just before serving. Serve with French bread crostini. Store leftovers in refrigerator up to 5 days.

Caramelized Onion, Bacon, & Gruyère Dip

SERVES 8

2 tablespoons olive oil

3½ cups chopped onions

1 teaspoon sugar

⅓ cup canola mayonnaise

⅓ cup light sour cream

3 bacon slices, cooked and crumbled

2 tablespoons chopped fresh chives, divided

¼ teaspoon salt

¼ teaspoon black pepper

2 ounces Gruyère cheese, shredded, plus 2 tablespoons for sprinkling on top

1) Swirl olive oil in medium pan; add onions. Cook on low for 20 minutes, sprinkle with sugar, and cook an additional 45 minutes to 1 hour. Stir occasionally so they don't burn.

2) Preheat oven to 425°.

3) In a medium bowl, combine mayonnaise, sour cream, bacon, 1 tablespoon chives, salt, and black pepper until well mixed.

4) Stir in shredded Gruyère and caramelized onions. Place in 1-quart baking dish, sprinkle 2 tablespoons additional Gruyère on top, and bake 20 minutes, or until bubbly.

5) Sprinkle with remaining 1 tablespoon chives, and serve warm with crostini or crackers.

Barbecue & Grilling

Homemade BBQ Sauce Favors

As you're preparing your menu, whip up extra batches of Homemade BBQ Sauce (page 51). Packaged creatively in a Mason jar with a basting brush, you have everything you need to award an informal "prize" to one or more of your guests. Frisbee champ at your summer picnic? Here's some sauce! Most loved potluck dish contributed for the day? Sauce for you, too!

BBQ Country Ribs

SERVES 6–8

Tender and juicy, these easy ribs are a potluck's best friend. Just be sure to bring along some extra napkins.

4 pounds country-style pork ribs

1 large sweet Vidalia onion, sliced

1½ cups Sweet Baby Ray's barbecue sauce (or your personal favorite)

1 cup orange juice

1) Preheat oven to 300°. Arrange ribs in a 9x13-inch baking dish; top with onion.

2) Whisk together BBQ sauce and orange juice; pour over ribs and onion. Cover tightly with foil, and bake 3 hours.

3) Uncover ribs. Increase oven temperature to 350°, and bake 1 hour, turning once after 30 minutes. Remove ribs to a warm platter, cover, and let stand 15 minutes.

4) Spoon fat off sauce, and serve with ribs.

Don't Forget the Incidentals!

Common items you might want to consider packing for your outdoor soirée: insect repellent, sunscreen, hand sanitizer, condiments (salt and pepper for sure), extra napkins or paper towels, and possibly matches for lighting grills or birthday candles (one of the best reasons to picnic!) You might also want to have some bandages and antibacterial ointment on hand, just in case.

Bacon-Wrapped BBQ Burgers

SERVES 4

8 slices bacon

½ chopped cup sweet onion

2 teaspoons olive oil

½ cup Homemade BBQ Sauce (page 51)

1½ pounds ground beef

¼ teaspoon salt

¼ teaspoon black pepper

4 hamburger buns, toasted

1) Arrange bacon on a paper-towel-lined microwave safe plate; cover with another paper towel. Microwave on HIGH for 2 minutes or until edges begin to crinkle, and bacon is partially cooked. (Can be done ahead.)

2) Preheat grill on medium high heat. Combine onion and olive oil with ground beef, and shape into 4 patties, slightly indenting the centers. Wrap sides of each patty with 2 bacon slices, overlapping ends. Secure with a wooden toothpick. Sprinkle patties with salt and black pepper.

3) Grill hamburger patties, covered with grill lid, 5–6 minutes on each side. Turn and brush with barbecue sauce (either the homemade sauce or your own). Remove from grill, and let stand 4–5 minutes. Remove toothpicks, and serve on buns.

Go Team! Whether you're grilling burgers in your yard, at a picnic, or tailgating, why not upgrade from the usual plastic condiment containers? Arrange ketchup, mustard, pickles, etc. in small Mason jars. Be creative, adding different sauces or flavored mayo. Finish things off by crafting a team-inspired pennant banner.

Grilled Italian Sausage Sandwiches
with Skillet Peppers

Grilled Italian Sausage Sandwiches with Skillet Peppers

SERVES 6

6 Italian sausage links

1 (12-ounce) bottle dark beer (I use Guinness)

2 medium green bell peppers, thinly sliced

1 medium onion, thinly sliced

2 tablespoons olive oil

2 teaspoons minced garlic

¼ teaspoon salt

½ teaspoon black pepper

6 buns, split

6 slices provolone cheese, halved

1) Place sausages in a large saucepan; add beer, and bring to a boil. Reduce heat; cover, and simmer 8–10 minutes, or until sausages are no longer pink.

2) Meanwhile, in a large skillet, sauté bell peppers and onion in oil until tender. Add garlic, and cook a minute longer. Season with salt and black pepper.

3) Drain sausages, discarding beer. Grill sausages, covered, over medium heat 4–6 minutes, or until browned with grill marks, turning occasionally. Line each bun with cheese, add sausage, then peppers and onion.

Make Them Kabobs!

Preheat grill to high heat. Soak bamboo skewers in cold water for a few minutes to prevent burning. Slice sausage links into 3- to 4-inch pieces, and thread sausages, as well as chunks of peppers and onion, onto skewers. Brush with olive oil, and grill for about 7 minutes per side.

Grilled Molasses & Peach Salsa Chicken

SERVES 6–8

MOLASSES MARINADE:

¾ cup molasses

⅓ cup soy sauce

¼ cup canola oil

¼ cup fresh lemon juice

2 tablespoons Worcestershire

3 garlic cloves, minced

2 pounds boneless, skinless chicken breasts

PEACH SALSA:

4 ripe yellow peaches, peeled and chopped

2–3 tablespoons chopped sweet onion

2 jalapeños, chopped (stem, seeds, and ribs discarded)

Juice of 1 lemon

2 tablespoons chopped fresh mint

1 teaspoon sugar

Salt and black pepper to taste

1) **Molasses Marinade:** Place ingredients, except chicken, into a 2-gallon zipper freezer bag; seal, and shake to combine. Add chicken, and reseal bag. Marinate at least 4 hours.

2) **Peach Salsa:** Place ingredients in food processor; pulse a couple of times, leaving some small pieces, and not completely liquid.

3) Place salsa in a bowl, and cover. Let stand an hour before serving, to give ingredients time to meld.

4) Preheat grill to high. Remove chicken from marinade, discarding marinade. Grill chicken with lid closed 9–10 minutes on each side, or until temperature reaches 180° in center of each breast. Remove from grill, and let stand 10 minutes. Slice thinly against the grain. Season with salt and black pepper, and top with Peach Salsa.

Classic BBQ Chicken

SERVES 4

This Classic BBQ Chicken is what prompted me to stuff some into my BBQ Deviled Eggs (page 29). While I patiently waited for the chicken to smoke, visions of the best deviled eggs danced in my head. Straight outta the smoker and into the eggs they went, declaring that this chicken is a winner! Served alongside the eggs, they make the most delicious pair.

1 (3- to 4-pound) chicken, giblets removed

4 cups chicken broth

1 (2-ounce) packet dry ranch dressing mix

2 cups chicken rub of choice

3 cups apple juice

1) Rinse chicken inside and out, and dry thoroughly; place in a deep pan. Add broth mixed with ranch dressing mix; cover, and refrigerate overnight.

2) Preheat smoker to 250°.

3) Remove chicken from marinade, and generously apply rub to chicken. Place chicken, breast side up, in aluminum pan on a raised meat rack. Pour apple juice in pan under the meat rack.

4) Cook in smoker about 3 hours, or until breast meat reaches 165°. Remove chicken from smoker, and allow to rest in pan 20 minutes. Carve into individual pieces to serve.

Apple Cider Brown Butter Honey-Kissed Wings

SERVES 6

HONEY SAUCE:

¼ cup butter

¼ cup honey

1 tablespoon apple cider vinegar

WINGS:

2 pounds chicken wings

1½ tablespoons olive oil

1½ teaspoons salt

½ teaspoon black pepper

1) **Honey Sauce:** Cook butter in saucepan over medium-high heat 5 minutes, or until brown bits begin to form. Transfer to a small bowl, and cool 5 minutes.

2) Cook honey and vinegar in saucepan over medium heat, stirring often, about 2 minutes. Whisk in browned butter.

3) **Wings:** Preheat grill to medium-high heat. Toss wings in a large bowl with olive oil. Add salt and black pepper, and toss to coat.

4) Grill wings, covered, 25–30 minutes, until skin is crisp and wings are done, turning occasionally. Using a basting brush, generously brush wings with Honey Sauce.

Kickin' Cajun Kabobs

SERVES 4–6

8 bamboo skewers

2 medium onions, cut into 1-inch pieces

12 ounces shrimp, peeled and deveined

14 ounces sausage, sliced thick

2 boneless, skinless chicken breasts, cubed

2 cups diced bell pepper, cut into 1-inch pieces

2 cups cherry tomatoes

2 tablespoons Creole seasoning

1) Preheat grill to high heat. Soak bamboo skewers in cold water for a few minutes to prevent burning.

2) On each skewer, thread a piece of onion, tail of a shrimp, a piece of sausage (placing the skewer off-center to allow the shrimp to wrap around the sausage), then a chicken cube.

3) Thread more vegetables, another shrimp-sausage combination, chicken cube, followed by more vegetables, ending with either a piece of onion or a piece of bell pepper. Repeat until you run out of ingredients. Sprinkle with Creole seasoning.

4) Grill 5–6 minutes on each side, or until vegetables begin to soften, shrimp are no longer pink, and chicken is cooked through.

5) Serve with a scoop of Cajun rice.

Grilled Shrimp with Creole Butter Sauce

MAKES 7 SKEWERS

You know the phrase referring to potato chips that says, "Bet you can't eat just one!" Same principle applies to these spicy, buttery nuggets of goodness. I am willing to bet that it's downright impossible for you to eat just one.

CREOLE BUTTER SAUCE:

½ stick butter, melted

¼ teaspoon Creole seasoning

¼ teaspoon cayenne pepper

¼ teaspoon paprika

SHRIMP:

1 pound large raw shrimp, peeled and deveined

Salt and black pepper to taste

1) **Creole Butter:** Combine ingredients, and set aside.

2) Preheat grill to medium heat. Soak bamboo skewers (about 7) in cold water for a few minutes to prevent burning.

3) **Shrimp:** Lightly season shrimp with salt and black pepper. Place 4–5 shrimp on each skewer. Lightly spray grill with nonstick cooking spray, and add shrimp skewers. Grill 3–4 minutes on each side.

4) Remove shrimp to a platter, and brush with Creole Butter. Serve immediately.

Grilled Pineapple with Cinnamon Honey Drizzle

MAKES 8 SLICES

1 pineapple, peeled and cored, sliced

½ cup honey

1 teaspoon cinnamon

1) Grill pineapple slices over medium heat 5–10 minutes.

2) While pineapple is grilling, mix together honey (softened in the microwave for about 30 seconds) with cinnamon.

3) Drizzle grilled pineapple with cinnamon honey, and serve.

Homemade BBQ Sauce

MAKES 2 CUPS

1 (15-ounce) can tomato sauce

½ cup apple cider vinegar

⅓ cup honey

¼ cup tomato paste

¼ cup molasses

3 tablespoons Worcestershire

2 teaspoons liquid smoke

1 teaspoon smoked paprika

1 teaspoon garlic powder

½ teaspoon black pepper

½ teaspoon onion powder

½ teaspoon salt

1) Whisk all ingredients together in a medium saucepan. Bring to a simmer over medium-high heat. Reduce heat to medium low, and simmer, uncovered, 20 minutes, or until sauce has thickened slightly.

2) Use sauce immediately, or refrigerate in a Mason jar, covered, for up to 1 week.

Breads

Wrap Your Sandwiches Nice & Neat.

When planning a picnic, bring along food that doesn't require plates. Even these plain sandwiches look extra special when wrapped in strips of wax paper or parchment paper, and secured with a bit of kitchen string or baker's twine. Add fruit packed in disposable cups, along with a few cookies, and you're good to go—with easy cleanup, too!

Pumpkin Cheesecake Muffins

MAKES 24 MUFFINS

FILLING:

1 (8-ounce) package cream cheese, softened

¼ teaspoon vanilla extract

1 cup powdered sugar

MUFFINS:

3 cups all-purpose flour

1 teaspoon ground cinnamon

1 teaspoon ground nutmeg

1 teaspoon ground cloves

1 tablespoon plus 1 teaspoon pumpkin pie spice

1 teaspoon salt

1 teaspoon baking soda

4 large eggs

2 cups sugar

2 cups pumpkin purée

1 teaspoon vanilla extract

1¼ cups vegetable oil

TOPPING:

½ cup sugar

5 tablespoons flour

1½ teaspoons ground cinnamon

4 tablespoons cold unsalted butter, cut into pieces

1) **Filling:** Mix ingredients in medium bowl until smooth. Cover tightly with plastic wrap, and refrigerate.

2) **Muffins:** Preheat oven to 350°, and line muffin pans with paper liners.

3) In medium bowl, whisk flour, cinnamon, nutmeg, cloves, pumpkin pie spice, salt, and baking soda.

4) In bowl of electric mixer, combine eggs, sugar, pumpkin purée, vanilla, and oil. Mix on low speed until blended. With mixer on low, add flour mixture, mixing just until incorporated.

5) **Topping:** Whisk sugar, flour, and cinnamon in a small bowl. Add butter pieces, and cut in with a pastry blender or 2 knives until mixture is crumbly. Refrigerate.

6) **To assemble:** Fill each muffin cup with 2 tablespoons batter, just enough to cover the bottom of the liner. Spoon 1 tablespoon Filling into center of each. Add remaining batter to cover filling completely, dividing batter evenly. Sprinkle 1 tablespoon Topping on each.

7) Bake 20–25 minutes. Remove from pan, and cool completely on wire rack.

54

Pecan Pie Muffins

MAKES ABOUT 20 MUFFINS

If you've never had a Pecan Pie Muffin, you don't know what you're missing. It tastes exactly like it sounds—like a bite of pecan pie in muffin form—a pie that doesn't require a fork! Easily portable, the next time you're heading to a brunch, take along these muffins. Two bites of pure pleasure.

1 cup packed light brown sugar

1 cup chopped pecans

½ cup flour

1 stick butter, melted

2 eggs

1 tablespoon vanilla extract

1) Mix brown sugar, pecans, and flour in a mixing bowl.

2) In a separate bowl, whisk butter, eggs, and vanilla extract until well blended. Add to brown sugar mixture, and stir just until moistened.

3) Fill paper-lined miniature muffin cups about ⅔ full. Bake at 350° for 12–16 minutes, or until a toothpick comes out clean. Serve warm.

Bakery-Style
Chocolate Chip Muffins

Bakery-Style Chocolate Chip Muffins

MAKES 12 GIGANTIC MUFFINS

2½ cups all-purpose flour

1 tablespoon baking powder

1 teaspoon baking soda

½ teaspoon salt

1 cup sugar

¼ cup light brown sugar

½ cup butter, melted

2 eggs, beaten

1 tablespoon vanilla

1¼ cups buttermilk

1½ cups miniature chocolate chips

1) Preheat oven to 425°. Grease a 12-cup muffin pan with nonstick cooking spray.

2) In a large bowl, mix together flour, baking powder, baking soda, salt, and both sugars. Add melted butter, eggs, vanilla, and buttermilk; stir just until combined. Fold in chocolate chips.

3) Fill each muffin cup completely full (about a heaping ¼ cup).

4) Bake 5 minutes, then decrease temperature to 375°, and bake another 10–12 minutes. Muffins are done when toothpick inserted into center comes out clean.

5) Remove from oven, and let cool for 5–10 minutes in the pan before serving.

Think Outside the Box.

Think these muffins are in a fancy box created especially for picnic lunches? You'd be wrong! I simply lined the bottom of small leftover gift boxes with handmade fabric napkins for easy serving ware. No plates required!

Streusel-Topped Cinnamon Apple Banana Nut Muffins

MAKES 6 JUMBO MUFFINS

These muffins came about when I had overripe bananas, and wasn't in the mood for banana bread. I also had an apple on hand, and I thought, well, cinnamon goes really well with apple; let's add that, too. I had also eaten a muffin earlier that week at a coffee shop, and it had the most delicious streusel topping. Therefore, folks, I made a muffin with the longest name in history: Streusel-Topped Cinnamon Apple Banana Nut Muffins.

¼ cup butter, softened

½ cup sugar

1 egg

¾ cup mashed ripe banana

½ teaspoon vanilla extract

1 cup all-purpose flour

¾ teaspoon baking powder

¼ teaspoon salt

⅛ teaspoon baking soda

⅛ teaspoon ground cinnamon

1 apple, peeled, cored, diced

¼ cup chopped pecans

STREUSEL TOPPING:

½ cup all-purpose flour

½ teaspoon ground cinnamon

3 tablespoons cold unsalted butter, cut into pieces

¼ cup brown sugar

1) In small bowl, cream butter and sugar. Beat in egg, banana, and vanilla.

2) Combine flour, baking powder, salt, baking soda, and cinnamon. Add to creamed mixture just until moistened.

3) Fold in diced apple and pecans (or other nut of choice).

4) **Streusel Topping:** In separate bowl, mix flour and cinnamon. Cut in butter with a pastry blender or fork until it resembles coarse crumbs. Stir in brown sugar.

5) Coat jumbo-size muffin pan with cooking spray, or use paper liners; fill ⅔ full with batter. Top batter with about 2 tablespoons Streusel Topping. May add more or less topping, depending on how much "crumble" you want on top.

6) Bake at 350° for 25–28 minutes, or until toothpick inserted in center comes out clean. Cool 5 minutes before removing from pan to a wire rack. Serve warm.

Strawberry Shortcake Muffins

MAKES 12 MUFFINS

2 cups all-purpose flour

2 teaspoons baking powder

¾ cup sugar

1 stick cold butter, cut into cubes

1 egg

1 teaspoon vanilla

1 cup heavy cream

1½ cups diced fresh strawberries

Powdered sugar, for dusting

1) Preheat oven to 350°. Grease or line 12 muffin cups with paper liners.

2) In a large bowl, whisk together flour, baking powder, and sugar. Cut in cold butter with a pastry blender (or two knives) until small pea-size pieces.

3) In a small bowl, mix together egg, vanilla, and cream. Add this mixture all at once to flour mixture. Stir with a spoon just until blended. Gently mix in strawberries.

4) Spoon batter into prepared muffin cups, making sure each muffin has some strawberries in it, and bake 22–25 minutes, or until a tester inserted in center comes out clean. Cool completely in pan before removing, as they are very soft while warm. Sprinkle with powdered sugar once cooled.

Glazed Lemon Blueberry Muffins

MAKES 12 MUFFINS

⅔ cup sugar

Zest of 1 lemon

½ cup butter, softened

2 eggs

1 teaspoon vanilla

¼ cup sour cream

2 tablespoons milk

2 cups all-purpose flour

2 teaspoons baking powder

¼ teaspoon salt

1½ cups fresh blueberries
   (may substitute frozen)

GLAZE:

2 tablespoons lemon juice

1 cup powdered sugar

1–2 teaspoons milk (more or
   less, as needed)

1) Preheat the oven to 350°. Line a muffin pan with paper liners, and set aside.

2) In a large bowl, or bowl of stand mixer, combine sugar and lemon zest. Add butter, eggs, vanilla, sour cream, and milk; mix to combine.

3) Add flour, baking powder, and salt; mix until just combined. Gently fold in blueberries.

4) Spoon into prepared muffin tins, filling ¾ full. Bake 18–20 minutes, or until lightly brown on top, and toothpick inserted into center comes out clean. Allow to cool 10 minutes.

5) **Glaze:** Whisk together all ingredients, adding enough milk to make a glaze that easily runs off the back of a spoon. Dip tops of muffins into Glaze, then let cool completely.

Sweet Strawberry Bread

MAKES 2 LOAVES

STRAWBERRY FROSTING:

1 pint fresh strawberries

1 (8-ounce) package cream cheese, softened

2 tablespoons powdered sugar

BREAD:

3 cups all-purpose flour

2 cups sugar

1 tablespoon cinnamon

1 teaspoon baking soda

1 teaspoon salt

1¼ cups vegetable oil

4 eggs, lightly beaten

1) **Strawberry Frosting:** Wash and drain strawberries, remove stems, then process in a food processor until smooth. (Strain to remove seeds, if desired). In a stand mixer, beat cream cheese with powdered sugar until smooth, then add 3 tablespoons puréed strawberries. Refrigerate. Reserve remaining strawberry purée.

2) **Bread:** Mix flour, sugar, cinnamon, baking soda, and salt in a bowl. Make a well in center of flour mixture. Add reserved strawberry purée, oil, and eggs to the well, and combine thoroughly.

3) Spray each of 2 (4x8-inch) loaf pans, or 4 miniature loaf pans well with nonstick cooking spray. Equally divide batter among pans, and bake at 350° for 1 hour, or until a toothpick inserted in center comes out clean.

4) Cool in pans 10 minutes. Gently remove from pans, and cool completely on a wire rack. Prior to serving, frost tops of loaves with cream cheese spread.

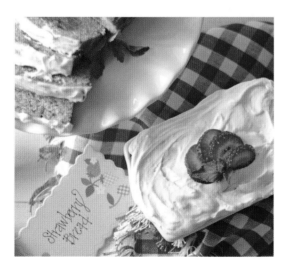

Sweet Onion Skillet Cornbread

SERVES 4–6

2 teaspoons vegetable oil

¼ cup butter

1 large Vidalia onion, chopped

1 (8-ounce) box Jiffy cornbread muffin mix

1 egg, beaten

⅓ cup whole milk

1 cup sour cream

1 cup grated sharp Cheddar cheese, divided

1) Preheat oven to 350°. Grease a 10-inch cast-iron skillet with vegetable oil. Keep warm in oven while preparing cornbread mix.

2) Melt butter in a saucepan. Add onion, and cook about 5 minutes, until tender. Remove from heat.

3) In a mixing bowl, combine cornbread mix, onion, egg, milk, sour cream, and ½ cup cheese. Carefully remove skillet from oven, and pour batter into hot pan. Top with remaining ½ cup cheese. Bake about 30 minutes, or until a toothpick inserted into middle comes out clean.

Mason Jar Cornbread Pies

If you like cornbread with your chili, consider layering in some of this Sweet Onion Skillet Cornbread instead of Fritos in your Homemade Chili Mason Jar Frito Pies (page 123)—it's perfect for tailgating!

Easy Yeast Rolls

MAKES ABOUT 18 ROLLS

1 cup milk

2 sticks butter, divided

1 (0.25-ounce) packet active dry yeast

¼ cup plus 2 tablespoons warm water, divided

⅓ cup plus 1 teaspoon sugar, divided

3 eggs, beaten

1 teaspoon salt

4½ cups all-purpose flour

Make Ahead!

These can be made a day ahead and served at room temperature, or to serve warm, wrap in foil and heat in 325° oven for 10–15 minutes.

1) In small saucepan, bring milk to a boil. Add 1 stick butter, turn off heat, and allow butter to melt completely. Cool to room temperature (may refrigerate).

2) In small bowl, dissolve yeast in 2 tablespoons warm water with 1 teaspoon sugar. Set aside until mixture is foamy.

3) In large mixer bowl, combine eggs with remaining ⅓ cup sugar. Mix in cooled milk mixture, proofed yeast, and salt to combine.

4) Add flour, 1 cup at a time, beating constantly with a mixer. Cover bowl with a towel, and allow to rise until double in size (about 1 hour).

5) Punch dough down, and form into small balls about ½ inch in size. Dough will be sticky.

6) Melt remaining 1 stick butter, and dip each ball into butter. Place 3 buttered balls into each muffin tin to form cloverleaf rolls. Let rise until double (15–30 minutes).

7) Bake at 350° about 12 minutes, or until golden brown. Cool slightly before serving.

Right-in-the-Skillet Biscuits

MAKES 10 BISCUITS

2 cups Bisquick

1 cup sour cream

**¼ cup lemon-lime soda
(such as 7-Up or Sprite)**

2 tablespoons butter, melted

1) Preheat oven to 375°.

2) In a large bowl, combine Bisquick and sour cream using a pastry blender. Add soda, a little at a time, and mix with a fork until dough forms a ball.

3) Turn dough out onto floured surface, and knead to incorporate. Add additional Bisquick as needed until dough is no longer sticky. With a floured rolling pin, roll dough to about ½-inch thickness.

4) Cut out biscuits using a round biscuit cutter, or rim of a juice glass. (Dipping your biscuit cutter into flour before cutting will help prevent it from sticking.)

5) Dip both sides of each biscuit into melted butter, then place close together in 10- to 12-inch cast-iron skillet. Bake 20 minutes, or until golden brown. Serve right from the skillet.

Fried Green Tomato BLT's with Aïoli Sauce

SERVES 1

1 medium-size green tomato, sliced ¼ inch thick

½ cup buttermilk

3 strips bacon

¼ cup all-purpose flour

¼ cup cornmeal

1 teaspoon Creole seasoning

Oil, for frying

2 slices bread

1 tablespoon aïoli sauce

2 leaves lettuce

1) Soak green tomato slices in buttermilk for at least 30 minutes at room temperature.

2) Fry bacon, and set aside, retaining grease in the pan.

3) Mix flour, cornmeal, and Creole seasoning in a wide shallow dish.

4) Pull tomato slices out of buttermilk, and dredge them in cornmeal mixture.

5) Fry tomato slices in oil over medium heat until golden brown on both sides, about 3–4 minutes per side; drain on paper towels.

6) Spread bread with aïoli sauce. Top with tomatoes and lettuce.

Spicy Avocado Bacon & Egg Sandwich Stackers

Spicy Avocado Bacon & Egg Sandwich Stackers

SERVES 6–8

AVOCADO SPREAD:

2 avocados

¼ cup sour cream

1 teaspoon salt

¾ teaspoon ground coriander

½ teaspoon chili powder

¼ teaspoon cayenne

Juice of 1 lime

SANDWICH STACKERS:

1 loaf thick-sliced sandwich bread

1 pound deli-sliced turkey (or other sandwich meat of your choice)

1 pound Cheddar cheese, sliced

1 pound sliced bacon, cooked

6 hard-boiled eggs, thinly sliced

Romaine lettuce

1) **Avocado Spread:** Scoop avocado flesh into bowl of food processor. Add remaining spread ingredients, and pulse until smooth. Adjust seasonings, if necessary. Refrigerate until ready to serve.

2) **Sandwich Stackers:** Lightly toast bread slices (they hold up better than untoasted bread). For each stack, add turkey and cheese to a slice of bread. Top with a second slice of bread, and spread with avocado mixture. Place egg and bacon slices on top. Top with a third slice of bread. Cut sandwich in half, and wrap with parchment paper for easy handling and presentation. Repeat for remaining stackers.

Keep It Neat.

Once you get your stackers all stacked, wrap them in wax paper cut to size (brown paper will work, too!), then place a toothpick through them to keep them in place for easy displaying and serving.

Breakfast & Brunch

Picnic Tablecloth Weights

Nothing wrecks an outdoor picnic more than a gust of wind sending your tablecloth edges flailing. Combat Mother Nature with some DIY (Do It Yourself) picnic tablecloth weights—simply purchase some large metal washers from the hardware store, spray paint them, tie on a ribbon, and attach to the corners of your tablecloth with safety pins. Guaranteed to stay put! Go crazy and color coordinate your weights with your picnic decor.

Breakfast Scramble Muffins

MAKES 12 MUFFINS

3 cups frozen hash browns, thawed

3 tablespoons melted butter

⅛ teaspoon salt

½ teaspoon black pepper, divided

½ pound bulk pork sausage

6 eggs

½ cup chopped onion

¼ cup chopped green pepper

¼ teaspoon garlic powder

1 cup shredded Cheddar cheese

Chopped green onions for garnish

1) Preheat oven to 400°.

2) In a bowl, combine hash browns, butter, salt, and ¼ teaspoon black pepper. Press mixture into bottom and up sides of greased muffin cups. Bake 12 minutes or until lightly browned.

3) In a large skillet, cook sausage over medium heat until no longer pink; drain.

4) In a large bowl, beat eggs. Add onion, green pepper, garlic powder, and remaining ¼ teaspoon black pepper. Stir in sausage and cheese.

5) Spoon by ⅓ cupfuls into muffin cups over hash browns. Bake 15–20 minutes, or until set, and a knife inserted near center comes out clean.

Skillet Breakfast Potatoes

SERVES 4–6

2 tablespoons butter

1 tablespoon oil

1½ pounds russet baking potatoes (about 3 large), scrubbed, dried, cubed

1 teaspoon seasoned or regular salt

¼ teaspoon black pepper

½ teaspoon garlic powder

½ teaspoon paprika

½ yellow onion, diced

1) Melt butter with oil in a large nonstick (or cast-iron) skillet over medium heat. Arrange potatoes evenly in skillet. Cover, and cook 10 minutes, turning potatoes once or twice.

2) Remove lid, season with salt, black pepper, garlic powder, and paprika. Stir to coat potatoes evenly with seasonings, then add onion on top of potatoes. Replace lid, and cook 5 minutes, stirring occasionally.

3) Remove lid and cook, uncovered, until potatoes are tender on the inside and crispy on the outside, 10–15 minutes. Remove from heat, and serve warm.

Bacon & Cheese Grits

SERVES 8–10

1½ cups grits, uncooked

3 cups grated Cheddar cheese, divided

3 eggs, beaten

⅓ cup milk

¼ teaspoon cayenne pepper

5 slices bacon, cooked, crumbled, divided

1) Preheat oven to 375°. Cook grits according to package directions; remove from heat. Add 2 cups cheese, eggs, milk, cayenne pepper, and 3 slices crumbed bacon; stir well.

2) Pour into greased 3-quart baking dish. Top with remaining 1 cup cheese and 2 slices cooked, crumbled bacon. Bake 20 minutes.

Crawfish Boil
Omelets

Crawfish Boil Omelets

SERVES 4

Here on the bayou, we love our crawfish boils. And when I say we "love" them, I mean we practically highlight crawfish boil season on the calendar, and count down the days just like anxiously awaiting Christmas. Because crawfish are in the height of their season around Easter, I grew up celebrating Easter Sundays with crawfish boils. You returned from church, changed your clothes, and got down to business. If you're lucky enough to have leftover crawfish, potatoes, and corn from a boil, make these omelets. You won't be disappointed. And if shrimp boils are more your speed, use those!

6 eggs

2 tablespoons milk

¼ teaspoon salt

¼ cup diced cooked red potato

¼ cup diced andouille sausage

¼ cup crawfish tails

¼ cup corn kernels (preferably leftover from boil)

4 mushrooms, sliced

1 tablespoon butter

2 tablespoons shredded Cheddar cheese

2 green onions, sliced

NOTE: You can make one giant omelet and cut into 4 equal parts, or you can divide the egg mixture and make individual omelets.

1) Whisk together eggs, milk, and salt in a medium bowl.

2) Combine potato, andouille, crawfish tails, corn, and mushrooms in a small bowl. If they have been refrigerated, warm in microwave.

3) Heat large nonstick skillet over medium heat; melt butter, and add egg mixture. Tilt pan so eggs spread out evenly.

4) Once eggs begin to set on bottom, one section at a time, lift up edge of omelet with a rubber spatula, and let uncooked egg run underneath.

5) When omelet is mostly set, sprinkle crawfish mixture evenly on one side of omelet.

6) Sprinkle cheese and green onion on top of crawfish mixture. When omelet is almost all the way set, fold in half, and remove from heat.

Praline French Toast Casserole

SERVES 6–8

Mornings are so much sweeter when they begin with this rich and decadent treat. Good things come to those who wait, though, and you'll need to allow this little guy to soak overnight before you're able to indulge.

8 eggs

1½ cups half-and-half

1 tablespoon plus ¾ cup packed brown sugar, divided

2 teaspoons vanilla extract

8 thick slices sourdough bread

1 stick butter

½ cup maple syrup

¾ cup chopped pecans

Whipped cream (optional)

1) Beat eggs and half-and-half in a small bowl. Whisk in 1 tablespoon brown sugar and vanilla extract. Pour ½ the egg mixture into a lightly greased 9×13-inch baking dish. Arrange bread slices in dish, trimming crusts to fit, if necessary. Pour remaining egg mixture over bread. Chill, covered, for several hours or overnight.

2) Melt butter, then stir in maple syrup and remaining ¾ cup brown sugar. Pour butter mixture into another 9×13-inch baking dish. Sprinkle pecans over the bottom. Place egg-soaked bread slices carefully on top of pecans with a spatula. Pour any egg mixture remaining in dish over bread. Bake at 350° for 30–35 minutes, or until bread is light brown and puffed.

3) To serve, invert toast onto plates, spoon pecans from bottom of dish over toast. Top with whipped cream, if desired.

Banana Split French Toast with Homemade Crème Fraîche

SERVES 4–6

CRÈME FRAÎCHE:
1 cup heavy whipping cream
1 tablespoon vanilla extract
⅓ cup powdered sugar
Pinch of salt

FRENCH TOAST:
6 eggs
¾ cup heavy whipping cream
1 tablespoon each: vanilla extract and cinnamon
1 teaspoon each: nutmeg and fine sea salt
4 ounces cream cheese, softened
¾ cup powdered sugar
1 loaf French bread
Butter, for frying

BANANAS:
1 stick butter
1 tablespoon vanilla extract
1 cup brown sugar
¼ cup cocoa powder
1 bunch bananas, sliced
Splash of dark rum
Vanilla ice cream
Maraschino cherries

1) **Crème Fraîche:** Combine all ingredients in chilled mixing bowl. Using a stand mixer, beat until stiff peaks form. Keep in an airtight container for up to 3 days.

2) **French Toast:** In a large mixing bowl, whisk together eggs, cream, vanilla, cinnamon, nutmeg, salt, cream cheese, and powdered sugar.

3) Cut French bread into 1-inch thick slices. Heat pan on medium high with a tablespoon of butter. Dip bread into egg mixture 20 seconds, and place into pan. Reduce heat to medium. Cook 2 minutes on each side. Remove from heat. Wipe pan clean between each bread slice.

4) **Bananas:** Melt butter in a skillet on high. Whisk in vanilla, brown sugar, and cocoa powder. Add bananas, and toss gently. Add rum, and flambé the pan. Once flame is gone, remove from heat.

5) Pour banana mixture over French toast. Top with a scoop of ice cream, Crème Fraîche, and cherries.

Chicken & Pecan Waffle
Sandwich Bites

Chicken & Pecan Waffle Sandwich Bites

SERVES 6–8

PECAN WAFFLES:

2 cups all-purpose flour, sifted

3 teaspoons baking powder

¼ teaspoon salt

¾ cup chopped pecans

2 eggs, separated

1½ cups milk

6 tablespoons butter, melted

CHICKEN:

1 pound chicken tenderloins, cut into bite-size pieces

2 tablespoons Creole seasoning

1 egg

¼ cup milk

1 cup all-purpose flour

¼ teaspoon black pepper

¼ teaspoon dry mustard

Vegetable oil

HONEY BUTTER:

½ cup butter, softened

¼ cup honey

¼ teaspoon cinnamon

1) **Pecan Waffles:** Sift together flour, baking powder, and salt; add pecans. In separate bowl, beat egg yolks until fluffy; combine with milk and melted butter. Add to flour mixture, mixing just until smooth.

2) Beat egg whites with electric mixer until stiff, and fold into batter. Cook waffles in hot waffle iron. Keep waffles warm in a 200° oven until ready to serve.

3) **Chicken:** Toss chicken in Creole seasoning. Whisk egg and milk together in a shallow bowl. Combine flour, black pepper, and mustard in another bowl.

4) Working in batches, dip seasoned chicken into egg mixture, then into flour mixture. Place chicken on a wire rack lined with paper towels, and allow to rest.

5) Heat 1 inch vegetable oil to 340 degrees in a deep fryer. Fry chicken until golden brown and crispy, about 5 minutes. Drain.

6) **Honey Butter:** Beat all ingredients with electric hand mixer until fluffy. Refrigerate.

7) **To assemble:** Cut each waffle into 4 squares; top with a piece of chicken and a dollop of Honey Butter, then add another waffle square. Hold together with a skewer or toothpick.

Casseroles

Let the Good Times Roll!

Portable and practical, wagons provide an easy way of rolling your supplies from vehicle to destination. Use them to elevate your food at picnics, display beverages at tailgates, or hold extra supplies at barbecues. *Laissez les bon temps rouler!*

Baked Potato Casserole for a Crowd

SERVES 8–10

If there were Academy awards given for potluck dishes, this Baked Potato Casserole would be a winner. The acceptance speech would sound something like, "I owe it all to the potatoes who have supported me. To the massive amount of cheese—you have been with me every step of the way. And lastly, to you, bacon—you complete me." Sorry to be so cheesy, but I think you get the picture. This casserole is good!

5 pounds red potatoes, cooked, cubed

1 pound sliced bacon, cooked and crumbled, divided

1 pound Cheddar cheese, cubed

1 large onion, finely chopped

1 cup mayonnaise

1 cup sour cream

1 tablespoon chopped chives

1 teaspoon salt

½ teaspoon black pepper

2 cups shredded Cheddar cheese

1) In a large bowl, combine potatoes and crumbled bacon (reserve ¼ cup for topping).

2) In another large bowl, combine cubed cheese, onion, mayonnaise, sour cream, chives, salt, and black pepper. Add to potato mixture, tossing gently to coat.

3) Transfer to a greased 4½-quart baking dish. Top with shredded cheese and remaining crumbled bacon.

4) Bake, uncovered, at 325° for 50–60 minutes. Casserole will be bubbly and lightly browned. Garnish with additional chives, if desired.

Tater Tot Casserole

SERVES 6–8

2 pounds lean ground beef

2 cups frozen mixed vegetables, thawed

1 teaspoon salt

¼ teaspoon black pepper

2 teaspoons Italian seasoning

1 (10¾-ounce) can cream of mushroom soup

½ cup sour cream

2 cups shredded Cheddar cheese, divided

1 (32-ounce) bag frozen tater tots, thawed

1) Preheat oven to 350°. Lightly coat 9x13-inch baking dish with cooking spray.

2) In large skillet, cook ground beef over medium-high heat until browned. Stir in mixed vegetables, salt, black pepper, and Italian seasoning. Cook 5 minutes, stirring often. Transfer to baking dish.

3) In medium bowl, whisk together soup and sour cream. Spread over beef mixture. Sprinkle with 1 cup cheese. Layer with tater tots.

4) Bake 40 minutes. Sprinkle remaining 1 cup cheese over the top, and continue baking until cheese is bubbly and beginning to brown, about 10 minutes.

Sweet Potato Casserole with Toasted Marshmallows

SERVES 6–8

This casserole is a combination of my mother's recipe for Sweet Potato Boats, adding heavy cream, plus whipping the potatoes similar to a soufflé. Like her "boats," it includes marshmallows and streusel topping, making them perfect for your sweet tooth. Just be sure to take the extra step and use fresh sweet potatoes...canned just aren't the same.

4–5 pounds sweet potatoes, peeled and cut into 2-inch pieces

2 eggs

1½ teaspoons vanilla

1 stick butter, melted

1 cup brown sugar

2–3 teaspoons salt, or to taste

½ cup heavy cream or milk

TOPPING:

½ cup brown sugar

⅓ cup all-purpose flour

⅓ cup butter, melted

1 cup chopped pecans

3–4 cups mini marshmallows

1) Cook sweet potatoes in enough water to cover in a saucepan until tender; drain. Beat with electric mixer in a mixing bowl until smooth.

2) Add eggs, vanilla, butter, brown sugar, salt, and cream; mix until smooth. (I like my potatoes to have a bit of texture, so I don't whip them long).

3) Spread potato mixture in bottom of greased 9x13-inch baking dish.

4) **Topping:** Combine brown sugar, flour, butter, and pecans in a bowl; mix well. Sprinkle mixture over potatoes. Bake in 375° oven, uncovered, 15–20 minutes, until pecans are caramelized.

5) Spread marshmallows evenly over pecan mixture. Return to oven for 5 minutes, or until marshmallows are puffy and lightly browned. Serve immediately.

Butternut Squash Lasagna

SERVES 6–8

1 (8-ounce) package lasagna noodles

1 tablespoon olive oil

1 pound spicy Italian sausage, casings removed

1 large yellow onion, chopped

2 garlic cloves, minced

1 (1½-pound) butternut squash, cut into ½-inch cubes

Salt and black pepper to taste

1 (15-ounce) container ricotta cheese

2 large eggs

1 (10-ounce) package frozen, chopped spinach, thawed and squeezed dry

2 cups shredded mozzarella cheese

1 cup fresh basil leaves, torn, or 3 teaspoons dried basil

6 cups tomato sauce

1) Preheat oven to 400°. Cook lasagna noodles according to package directions. Drain, and set aside.

2) Heat olive oil in a large skillet over medium-high heat. Add sausage, and cook until browned, about 5 minutes. Drain on paper towels.

3) Add onion and garlic to pan, adding more olive oil, if necessary. Cook 1 minute. Add squash, and cook until tender. Season with salt and black pepper. Remove from heat, and drain excess liquid. Stir in sausage.

4) In a medium bowl, whisk together ricotta, eggs, spinach, and a bit more salt and black pepper.

5) Spread ⅓ of the tomato sauce in 9x13-inch casserole dish. Arrange a layer of lasagna noodles on top. Evenly distribute ⅓ of the ricotta mixture over noodles. Sprinkle with ⅓ of the mozzarella, and ⅓ of the basil. Repeat to make more layers, ending with cheese on top.

6) Cover dish with foil, and bake 30 minutes. Remove foil, and bake 10–15 minutes longer, until golden brown and bubbly. Let cool at least 10 minutes before serving.

Eggplant Dressing

Eggplant Dressing

SERVES 6–8

Years ago, my Great Aunt Polly sent me home with a container of her eggplant dressing that changed the way I will forever look at eggplants. The eggplants were barely noticeable, cooked down and nestled within the familiar dressing that I've loved all my life. I won't be telling my mother that my heart belongs to another, but I will be requesting my Aunt Polly's eggplant recipe. This recipe was derived from my newfound love of eggplants.

1½ pounds ground beef

1 large onion, chopped

1 green bell pepper, chopped

2 medium-size eggplants, peeled and chopped

1 cup chicken broth

Salt and black pepper to taste

1 cup cooked rice

1 bunch green onions, chopped

1) Brown ground beef in a large heavy-bottomed pot, or a cast-iron skillet. Drain fat, if necessary.

2) Add onion and bell pepper; cook, stirring often, until wilted, about 5 minutes.

3) Add eggplant and broth; simmer until eggplant is very tender and soft. Gently mash with the back of a spoon. Season with salt and black pepper. Add rice and green onions, and combine well.

Sausage Macaroni & Cheese Casserole

SERVES 6–8

1 pound elbow macaroni

2 tablespoons olive oil, divided

1 pound andouille sausage, cut into ½-inch rounds

1 medium onion, chopped

1 green bell pepper, chopped

Salt and black pepper to taste

1 clove garlic, minced

1 tablespoon all-purpose flour

1½ cups whole milk

4 ounces cream cheese, softened

2 teaspoons Creole seasoning

8 ounces sharp Cheddar cheese, shredded or cubed

8 ounces Colby Jack cheese, shredded or cubed

1) Heat oven to 425°. Grease a shallow 3-quart baking dish or 6 (2-cup) ramekins. Cook macaroni according to package directions.

2) Heat 1 tablespoon olive oil in large skillet over medium-high heat. Add sausage, and brown, about 1 minute per side. Remove from skillet and set aside.

3) Add remaining 1 tablespoon oil to skillet, and heat over medium-low heat. Add onion, bell pepper, salt, and black pepper. Cover and cook, stirring occasionally, until very tender, 8–10 minutes.

4) Stir in garlic, and cook 1 minute. Sprinkle flour over mixture, and cook, stirring constantly, about 1 minute.

5) Whisk in milk; bring to a simmer. Whisk in cream cheese and Creole seasoning until blended. Stir in Cheddar and Colby Jack cheeses, and simmer, stirring occasionally, until melted, 1–2 minutes.

6) Toss macaroni with sauce, fold in sausage, and transfer to prepared baking dish. Bake until golden brown, 10–12 minutes.

Chicken Pot Pie Casserole

SERVES 6–8

Is there any food more comforting than chicken pot pie? Well, yes, yes there is. Chicken Pot Pie Casserole! Your favorite comfort food made into a casserole makes it a perfect choice for potlucks.

½ stick butter, melted

1½–2 pounds boneless, skinless chicken breasts, cooked and cubed

1½ teaspoons dried sage, divided

1½ teaspoons dried thyme, divided

½ teaspoon freshly ground black pepper

2 cups frozen mixed vegetables, unthawed

½ cup finely chopped sweet onion

2 cups Bisquick

¼ teaspoon onion powder

1½ cups whole milk

1 cup chicken broth

1 (10¾-ounce) can cream of chicken soup, undiluted

1 cup shredded Cheddar cheese

1) Preheat oven to 375°. Pour melted butter into 9x13-inch glass casserole dish, evenly coating the bottom.

2) Arrange chicken evenly in bottom of casserole dish. Sprinkle with 1 teaspoon sage, 1 teaspoon thyme, then black pepper. Top with frozen mixed vegetables and onion.

3) Whisk together Bisquick, onion powder, and remaining ½ teaspoon sage and ½ teaspoon thyme. Using a large dinner fork, stir in milk just until combined. Slowly pour over chicken and vegetable mix.

4) Whisk together chicken broth and chicken soup until combined. Slowly pour evenly over Bisquick mixture.

5) Finally, top with Cheddar cheese. Bake 35–40 minutes, or until top is golden brown.

Cajun Chicken Pasta Casserole

Cajun Chicken Pasta Casserole

SERVES 4–6

1 (12-ounce) package bow tie pasta

1 pound boneless, skinless chicken breasts, cubed

Olive oil, enough to coat pan

1 bunch green onions, chopped

1 medium green bell pepper, chopped

1 medium sweet red bell pepper, chopped

½ (14½-ounce) can reduced-sodium chicken broth

1 (10¾-ounce) can condensed cream of chicken soup

½ (10¾-ounce) can condensed cream of mushroom soup

½ cup milk

1½ teaspoons Creole seasoning

1 teaspoon garlic powder

½ teaspoon black pepper

1½ cups shredded Colby Jack cheese

1) Preheat oven to 350°. Cook pasta according to package instructions; drain and set aside.

2) In a Dutch oven, sauté chicken in olive oil until juices run clear. Remove with a slotted spoon, and set aside.

3) In same pan, sauté onions and bell pepper until tender. Add broth, soups, milk, Creole seasoning, garlic powder, and black pepper. Bring to a boil; remove from heat. Add pasta and chicken, tossing to coat.

4) Pour chicken and pasta mixture into a greased 9x13-inch baking dish. Sprinkle with cheese; cover and bake an additional 20–25 minutes, or until cheese is golden and bubbly.

Pasta Alternatives:

I've used bow tie pasta in this recipe, but you can also use fettuccine or linguine, if you prefer.

Shrimp & Wild Rice Casserole

SERVES 6–8

3 cups long-grain wild rice

2 cups chicken stock

1 cup diced yellow onion

2 cups roughly diced green bell pepper

6 tablespoons butter

4 garlic cloves, minced

8 ounces mushrooms, sliced

2 cups sliced fresh or frozen okra

Juice from ½ lemon

1½ teaspoons salt

¼ teaspoon black pepper

½ teaspoon cayenne pepper, or to taste

2 pounds medium shrimp, peeled

1 (10¾-ounce) can cream of shrimp soup

1 cup grated white Cheddar cheese (optional)

½ cup grated Parmesan cheese

1) Cook rice according to package directions, replacing 2 cups water with chicken stock.

2) In a large pan, sauté onion and bell pepper in butter until wilted, about 5 minutes. Add garlic and mushrooms and cook another 3–4 minutes. Stir in okra, lemon juice, salt, black pepper, and cayenne pepper, and cook 5 minutes. Add shrimp, and cook about 3 minutes until shrimp turn pink. Do not overcook.

3) Add soup along with rice, and stir until blended completely. Stir in white Cheddar.

4) Pour into greased 9x13-inch casserole dish, top with Parmesan, and bake in 325° oven for 15–20 minutes, until bubbly and cheese is melted.

Shrimp & Okra Casserole with Creole Tomato Sauce

SERVES 6–8

3 strips bacon

1 tablespoon minced garlic

1 medium onion, diced

2 pounds Creole tomatoes,
cut in medium-size chunks

2 bay leaves

2 teaspoons chopped fresh
thyme

Salt and black pepper to taste

2 pounds fresh okra, tops
removed

1½–2 pounds medium shrimp,
peeled, deveined

1 tablespoon Creole
seasoning, or to taste

½ loaf French bread
(4–6 inches)

½ stick butter, melted

1) Dice bacon, and pan-fry in Dutch oven until crispy. Add garlic, onion, and tomatoes. Season with bay leaves, thyme, salt, and black pepper. Simmer 30–45 minutes.

2) Slice okra in half lengthwise, and layer bottom of 9x13-inch casserole dish, arranging each row with tips of okra filling empty space of last row. Place shrimp over okra in a single layer, and sprinkle with Creole seasoning. Remove bay leaves from tomato mixture, and pour over shrimp.

3) Cut or tear bread into pieces, and place in bowl of food processor. Pulse into ½ cup crumbs, and mix with melted butter. Sprinkle over top of casserole, and bake at 375° for 25–30 minutes, or until crumbs are golden brown and casserole is bubbly.

Slow Cooker

Stenciled Cutlery

Give your disposable wooden cutlery some extra pizzazz by stenciling (or vinyl'ing) BBQ onto your forks and sticking them right into your BBQ in a Jar (page 101). Your guests will think you're so creative!

Slow Cooker Meatloaf
in a Mason Jar

Slow Cooker Meatloaf

SERVES 6–8

I'm not really sure why meatloaf gets such a bad rap. To me, it embodies an old-time nostalgia of what a home-style meal should be. The fact that modern technology allows you to pop it into the crockpot to cook while you're away working or running errands is pure happiness! Serve with a side of mashed potatoes and a bit of sweet corn, and you've got a home-style meal with very little effort.

2 eggs

2 slices bread, cubed

2–3 teaspoons milk

2 pounds ground beef

1 onion, diced (about 1 cup)

Salt and black pepper to taste

½ cup ketchup

¼ cup brown sugar

1 tablespoon dry mustard

1) Beat eggs in a medium-size bowl; add bread cubes. Add milk to moisten bread.

2) Add ground beef, onion, salt, and black pepper. With your hands, work mixture until bread disappears. Place mixture into slow cooker, shaping to fit.

3) Combine ketchup, brown sugar, and dry mustard; spread sauce over top of meatloaf.

4) Cook 4–5 hours on LOW, or till meat thermometer reaches 160°.

Serve in a Mason jar!

Easy to transport and easy to serve, consider putting your cooked meatloaf in Mason jars. Layer with mashed potatoes for a tasty combination. Just prior to serving, add an additional layer of mashed potatoes garnished with chopped green onions, and watch your guests oooh and ahhh!

Slow Cooker Stuffed Bell Peppers

SERVES 6

Fix 'em and forget 'em...these stuffed peppers couldn't be easier. There's no need to cook the meat prior to stuffing the peppers, so they make the perfect addition to any party when you're busy running around getting ready.

6 large bell peppers

1 pound lean ground beef

½ cup chopped onion

1 bunch green onions, chopped

1 (14-ounce) can diced tomatoes

2 tablespoons Worcestershire

1 cup long-grain wild rice, cooked (any kind of rice will work)

1 teaspoon salt

1 teaspoon black pepper

1¼ cups shredded Cheddar cheese, divided

¼ cup water

1) Cut off top of each bell pepper, and scrape out seeds and membranes. Set aside.

2) Mix together ground beef, onion, green onions, diced tomatoes, Worcestershire, rice, salt, black pepper, and 1 cup cheese. Stuff each bell pepper with mixture.

3) Pour water in slow cooker, then place bell peppers in water. Cook on LOW 6 hours (or HIGH 4 hours) until bell peppers are tender, and ground beef is cooked through.

4) About 15 minutes before done, sprinkle with remaining ½ cup cheese.

For Festive Gatherings–

Choose bell peppers to coordinate with your theme. Red and green are perfect for a Christmas get-together, and red, green, and yellow complete the theme for Cinco de Mayo.

Homestyle Chicken & Dumplings

SERVES 6–8

I did an interview one time with a news station in Salt Lake City about my 52 Pies Project (a pie a week for the entire year). While chatting about pies, she also asked me about the one dish I couldn't live without. Nervous and on the spot, I blurted out crawfish étouffée, and chicken and dumplings. When I told my husband the story, he said, "I knew you liked chicken and dumplings, but did you really say you couldn't live without it"? Why, yes, yes, I did say that. And while I could live without them, who in the world would want to?

4 boneless, skinless chicken breasts, cut in strips

½ stick butter, sliced

1 medium onion, finely diced

2 (10¾-ounce) cans cream of chicken soup

1 (32-ounce) carton chicken broth

2 (10-ounce) cans flaky biscuits, torn into pieces

Salt, black pepper, and Creole seasoning to taste

1) Place chicken, butter, onion, and soup in slow cooker. Pour in chicken broth until completely covered.

2) Cover, and let cook 8–10 hours on LOW.

3) One hour before serving, place biscuit pieces in slow cooker. Cook until dough is no longer raw in center. Add seasonings to taste.

BBQ Pulled Pork

GO TEAM

Slow Cooker
BBQ Pulled Pork

Slow Cooker BBQ Pulled Pork

SERVES 6–8

2 medium yellow onions, thinly sliced

3 garlic cloves, minced

1 cup chicken stock

2 tablespoons dark brown sugar

1 tablespoon chili powder

1 tablespoon salt, or to taste

½ teaspoon ground cumin

½ teaspoon ground cinnamon

1 (4½- to 5-pound) boneless or bone-in pork shoulder (also known as pork butt), twine or netting removed

2 cups barbecue sauce (I use Sweet Baby Ray's Hickory & Brown Sugar)

6–8 buns (optional)

1) Place onion and garlic in bottom of slow cooker, and pour stock on top.

2) In small bowl, combine sugar, chili powder, salt, cumin, and cinnamon. Pat pork dry with paper towels, and rub spice mixture over pork, patting to keep it in place. Place in slow cooker on top of onions.

3) Cover, and cook on HIGH 6–8 hours, or on LOW 8–10 hours.

4) Once pork has finished cooking, remove to a cutting board to shred. If the pork has a bone, discard it.

5) Remove all but ½ cup liquid from slow cooker. Add shredded meat back to slow cooker with liquid. Add barbecue sauce.

6) Serve as a main meat dish, or as sandwiches.

Serve Sauce on the Side.

Alternately, offer barbecue sauce on the side, to allow guests to control the amount. Nice to provide a variety of flavors, so your guests can choose their own personal favorite.

Fiesta Chicken

SERVES 6–8

Say hello to the baked potato's new best friend.

1 pound boneless, skinless chicken breasts

2 (10-ounce) cans Mexican-style corn, undrained

1 (15-ounce) can black beans, drained

1 cup salsa

2 tablespoons taco seasoning

½ cup shredded Mexican blend cheese

Baked potatoes

Sour cream (optional)

1) Place chicken in slow cooker. Add corn, beans, salsa, and taco seasoning. Cook 4–6 hours on LOW.

2) During last 5 minutes, sprinkle in shredded cheese, and heat until melted. Serve over baked potatoes, and top with sour cream, if desired.

Fiesta Chicken Bar

Fiesta Chicken is also delicious served with Spanish rice, or wrapped inside warm tortillas. Set up as a buffet-style dinner, letting family or guests choose their favorite way to enjoy it. Include potatoes, rice, tortillas, and tortilla chips alongside toppings such as shredded cheese, sour cream, salsas, guacamole, chopped tomatoes, shredded lettuce, and sliced jalapeños.

Slow Cooker BBQ Chicken Sammies

SERVES 6

1 (3- to 3½-pound) whole chicken, cut up

2 teaspoons salt

1 teaspoon paprika

½ teaspoon garlic powder

½ teaspoon black pepper

½ cup cola soft drink

½ cup ketchup

¼ cup firmly packed light brown sugar

2 tablespoons apple cider vinegar

2 tablespoons bourbon

1 lemon, sliced

6 hoagie buns, sliced lengthwise

Creamy Homemade Coleslaw (page 141)

1) Place chicken in a single layer in a lightly greased 6-quart slow cooker.

2) Stir together salt, paprika, garlic powder, and black pepper in a small bowl. Sprinkle over chicken.

3) Whisk together cola, ketchup, brown sugar, vinegar, and bourbon in a small bowl, and slowly pour mixture between chicken pieces. Place lemon slices in a single layer on top of chicken.

4) Cover, and cook on HIGH 5 hours (or on LOW 6–7 hours), or until chicken is done and juices run clear.

5) Remove chicken from slow cooker, and let cool slightly, 10–15 minutes. Discard lemons. Skin, debone, and shred chicken using 2 forks.

6) Skim fat from pan juices, and drizzle juices over chicken.

7) Serve on hoagie buns, topped with Creamy Homemade Coleslaw.

BBQ in a Jar!

Instead of serving this chicken as a sandwich, layer it in a jar with baked beans and coleslaw, and top with cheese (see photo page 92).

Slow Cooker Red Beans & Rice

SERVES 6–8

My husband grew up in New Orleans, where it's tradition to eat Red Beans & Rice on Mondays, the customary wash day. A pot of red beans could cook all day, requiring little hands-on attention while laundry was done. This slow cooker version takes even less hands-on attention, and is a great way to start the week.

4 cups dried red beans

2½ teaspoons olive oil

1 large onion, diced

1 tablespoon garlic, minced

1 tablespoon Creole seasoning

1 teaspoon dried oregano

2 links hot andouille sausage, chopped

1 package pickled pork, chopped

3 cups chicken broth

1 teaspoon Tabasco

1 teaspoon red wine vinegar

Salt and black pepper to taste

3 cups cooked white rice

Green onion, chopped, for garnish

1) Soak beans overnight in enough water to cover by an inch. Drain, and rinse; set aside.

2) Heat olive oil in a heavy skillet; sauté onion until translucent. Add garlic, Creole seasoning, and oregano.

3) Add sausage, and cook until edges begin to brown, and are slightly crisping.

4) Put sausage mixture into slow cooker. Add drained beans, pork, chicken broth, Tabasco, vinegar, salt, and black pepper; stir to combine.

5) Cook on HIGH 6–8 hours, until beans are soft. After about 6 hours, stir, and using the back of a wooden spoon, gently mash some beans against the side, allowing them to dissolve into the liquid.

6) Serve with a scoop of white rice on top. Garnish with chopped green onion.

Slow Cooker Bread Pudding

SERVES 8–10

BREAD PUDDING:

3 large eggs

½ cup packed light brown sugar

2 tablespoons ground cinnamon

1 teaspoon ground nutmeg

1 cup milk

1 cup heavy cream

1¼ teaspoons vanilla extract

½ stick butter, melted

½ cup raisins

½ cup pecans

1 loaf French bread

GLAZE:

⅓ cup heavy cream

1 cup powdered sugar

1 stick butter

1½ tablespoons rum

1) **Bread Pudding:** Spray slow cooker lightly with nonstick cooking spray.

2) In a small bowl, whisk together eggs, brown sugar, cinnamon, and nutmeg. Stir in milk, heavy cream, vanilla, and butter. Fold in raisins and pecans.

3) Slice French bread into 1-inch cubes, and arrange in bottom of slow cooker. Pour egg mixture over top, making sure to moisten each piece of bread.

4) Cover, and cook on LOW 2 hours or until center is firm. Keep the lid on, and let stand 30 minutes.

5) **Glaze:** Combine all ingredients, except rum, in a saucepan on low heat. Stir until melted and well combined. Do not boil.

6) Add rum, and remove from heat. Spoon over Bread Pudding to serve.

Bucket O' Catfish Bites

Seafood

A Drop in the Bucket!

Skip the paper plates, and instead serve your bite-size catfish and hush puppies in inexpensive bucket pails. Line the buckets with parchment paper to keep things tidy. Not only are your buckets reusable, but they'll also function as decor.

Easy Crawfish Ètouffée

SERVES 6–8

Ètouffée is one of the signature dishes of South Louisiana, and one of my absolute favorites. While it is traditionally served over rice, it is incredibly delicious over fish, and even a baked potato. Don't worry if you live in an area where crawfish aren't available; this recipe will work with shrimp just as easily.

4 sticks butter

5 cups chopped onions

2 cups chopped celery

1 cup chopped green bell pepper

1 cup chopped red bell pepper

4 teaspoons salt

1½ teaspoons cayenne pepper

¼ cup all-purpose flour

½ cup cold water

4 pounds crawfish tails, deveined

2 teaspoons Tabasco

1 cup hot water

2 bunches green onions, chopped

6 cups hot cooked rice

1) Melt butter in a large saucepan or Dutch oven. Add onions, celery, and bell peppers. Sauté over medium heat until onions are tender and translucent. Add salt and cayenne pepper. Reduce heat to low, and simmer 1 hour, stirring occasionally.

2) Whisk flour into cold water. Stir into vegetables. Cook 3 minutes, or until thickened, stirring constantly.

3) Add crawfish, Tabasco, and hot water. Bring to a boil, then reduce heat to low; simmer 15–20 minutes. (Add more water, 1 tablespoon at a time, if the mixture is too thick.) Stir in green onions. Serve over rice.

Seafood au Gratin

SERVES 4–6

Rich and creamy, this comes with a warning: You may need your stretchy pants!

8 ounces crawfish tails

8 ounces peeled cooked shrimp

8 ounces lump crabmeat, shells removed

2 garlic cloves, minced

2 tablespoons butter

½ cup chicken broth

1 tablespoon liquid crab boil

1 teaspoon Creole seasoning

¾ cup milk

1 (8-ounce) jar Alfredo sauce

12 ounces Velveeta cheese, cubed

8 ounces noodles, cooked

2 cups shredded mozzarella cheese

1) Preheat oven to 350°. Sauté crawfish tails, shrimp, crabmeat, and garlic in butter in a skillet until seafood is heated through.

2) Stir in chicken broth, liquid crab boil, Creole seasoning, milk, Alfredo sauce, and Velveeta cheese. Cook over medium-low heat until cheese melts; stirring constantly.

3) Spread noodles in a greased 9x13-inch baking dish. Pour seafood sauce over noodles, and top with mozzarella cheese.

4) Bake about 20 minutes, until mozzarella cheese melts, and is bubbly.

Shrimp & Crabmeat Pasta

SERVES 4–6

1 stick butter

½ cup olive oil

2 garlic cloves, minced

1 pound raw medium shrimp, peeled

¾ cup chopped green onions

1½ cups half-and-half

¾ cup freshly grated Parmesan cheese

1 teaspoon cornstarch

¼ cup water

1 pound crabmeat

¾ cup chopped fresh parsley

Salt and black pepper to taste

1 (16-ounce) package angel hair pasta, cooked

1) Melt butter with olive oil in a skillet. Add garlic and shrimp, and sauté until shrimp turn pink.

2) Stir in green onions, half-and-half, and Parmesan cheese. Cook for several minutes, stirring constantly.

3) Dissolve cornstarch in water, and stir into shrimp mixture. Stir in crabmeat and parsley. Cook 5 minutes, or until completely heated through. Season with salt and black pepper.

4) Pour over angel hair pasta, tossing to coat. Serve immediately.

Shrimp Rolls

SERVES 4

1 teaspoon liquid crab boil

3 pounds medium shrimp, peeled and deveined

¾ cup mayonnaise

1 small bunch green onions, finely chopped

Juice of 2 lemons

¼ teaspoon celery salt

¼ teaspoon garlic salt

2 celery stalks, finely chopped

8 hoagie buns, split open

¼ cup butter, melted

1) Add crab boil to a large pot of water and bring to a boil. Add shrimp, and cook just until they turn pink and float to the top, 2–3 minutes. Remove shrimp, rinse with cold water, and drain. Transfer to a plate, and refrigerate until ready to use.

2) In a medium bowl, combine mayonnaise, green onions, lemon juice, celery salt, and garlic salt. Stir in shrimp and celery. Refrigerate at least 30 minutes.

3) Preheat a skillet to medium high heat. Brush insides of hoagie buns with melted butter, and put buns buttered side down on the skillet, toasting until golden brown.

4) Divide shrimp mixture evenly among buns.

Tin Foil Shrimp Boil

Tin Foil Shrimp Boil

SERVES 4

In the mood for a shrimp boil, but don't feel like dealing with all the mess? Here's your solution. This recipe will serve four, but is easily multiplied and only limited by how much room you have on the grill. The beauty is, the contents of the tin foil package can be devoured right inside its container. No mess. No fuss.

1 pound shell-on shrimp, deveined

2 teaspoons seafood seasoning (such as Zatarain's Shrimp & Crab Boil liquid concentrate)

6 small red potatoes, quartered

2 links andouille sausage, cut into ¼-inch slices

4 small pieces corn on cob

4 tablespoons butter

1 lemon, sliced into 8 rounds

Garlic bread wedges (optional)

1) Preheat grill to medium-high heat.

2) Toss shrimp with seafood seasoning in a small bowl. Place 2 (12-inch) sheets of heavy-duty aluminum foil per packet (8 sheets total for 4 packets) on a flat surface.

3) Divide ingredients among the 4 packets, layering in potatoes, sausage, shrimp, corn, butter, and lemon. Fold up ends of foil, and seal into packets.

4) Place packets on grill, cover, and cook until potatoes are done, and shrimp are pink, 15–20 minutes. Can be cooked in 350° oven for 30–40 minutes, if desired. Serve with garlic bread

New Orleans-Style Barbecue Shrimp

SERVES 6–8

Experiencing the New Orleans-Style Barbecue Shrimp is a bit of a production. It's a tad messy, because the beauty of the dish is in the spicy butter sauce. To serve, you'll supply both the shrimp and the extra "juice" in a bowl or shallow dish. French bread is accompanied, and it's one of the only times when sopping up the juice is not only allowed, but encouraged. If you can get past the mess, you're in for a special treat.

4 pounds unpeeled headless shrimp, rinsed, drained

½ teaspoon salt

4 teaspoons black pepper

2 teaspoons Creole seasoning

2 teaspoons Worcestershire

½ teaspoon garlic powder

4 sticks butter, melted

1 loaf French bread, sliced

1) Place shrimp in a Dutch oven, and cook over medium heat until shrimp turn pink, stirring constantly. Remove from heat.

2) Sprinkle with salt, black pepper, Creole seasoning, Worcestershire, and garlic powder. Pour melted butter over shrimp. Return to heat, and bring to a boil.

3) Reduce heat to medium, and cook 3–4 minutes, stirring occasionally. Remove from heat. Let stand, covered, for as long as possible to allow the butter to permeate the shrimp.

4) Serve with toasted French bread.

Crab Stuffed Baked Flounder

SERVES 4–6

1½ pounds flounder fillets

Salt to taste

1 medium onion, diced

2 cloves garlic, minced

2 tablespoons chopped celery

2 tablespoons chopped green bell pepper

2 tablespoons olive oil

1 teaspoon salt

½ teaspoon black pepper

⅛ teaspoon thyme

1 tablespoon chopped parsley

1 egg

¾ cup bread crumbs

1 cup crabmeat

1 stick butter, melted

1) Preheat oven to 375°.

2) Rinse fillets and pat dry. Sprinkle each with salt. Slice a large slit into side of each. Set aside.

3) Prepare stuffing by sautéing onion, garlic, celery, and bell pepper in olive oil.

4) In a small bowl, combine seasonings, egg, and bread crumbs. Mix in crabmeat and vegetable mixture until thoroughly combined.

5) Place a generous amount of stuffing into slit of each fillet. Generously brush each side of fillets with melted butter. Place in a lightly greased, shallow baking dish, cover, and bake 20 minutes.

6) Uncover, and bake an additional 5–10 minutes, or until fillets are golden and bubbly.

Hushpuppies
Bucket O' Catfish Bites shown on page 104

Bucket O' Catfish Bites with Hushpuppies

SERVES 6 • MAKES 2 DOZEN HUSHPUPPIES

2 cups vegetable oil

1 cup all-purpose flour

½ cup stone-ground cornmeal

2 tablespoons Creole seasoning

1 teaspoon onion powder

1 teaspoon garlic powder

½ teaspoon cayenne pepper

1 egg

2 pounds catfish nuggets, skin removed

Salt to taste

¼ cup lemon juice

HUSHPUPPIES:

1 cup yellow cornmeal

1 cup all-purpose flour

½ teaspoon baking powder

1 teaspoon sugar

1 teaspoon salt

Dash of Creole seasoning

1 egg, beaten

¾ cup milk

3 teaspoons minced sweet onion

1 quart or more vegetable oil

1) In heavy 3-quart saucepan, heat oil over medium-high heat to 375°.

2) In shallow dish, mix flour, cornmeal, Creole seasoning, onion powder, garlic powder, and cayenne pepper. In another shallow dish, beat egg with fork until foamy.

3) Sprinkle catfish nuggets with salt and lemon juice. Dip each nugget into beaten egg, then roll in flour mixture to coat. Drop 4–6 nuggets at a time into hot oil. Cook 2 minutes, then turn, and cook 1 minute longer or until deep golden brown. Remove from oil; drain on paper towels.

4) **Hushpuppies:** Mix cornmeal, flour, baking powder, sugar, salt and Creole seasoning in a large bowl. Add egg, milk, and onion, and stir until well blended.

5) Drop one heaping teaspoon at a time into hot, 350° oil (you can use the same oil as the fish, just replenish and bring back to temperature). Fry until golden brown. Drain on a paper towel-lined plate. Serve in a basket with fish and tarter sauce.

Main Dish Meats

Elevate your Tailgate

Ready to elevate your tailgate? Consider serving your chili as Mason Jar Frito Pies. Because you'll be eating directly from the jar, you've eliminated the need for multiple serving containers as well.

Beer Can Chicken

SERVES 4–6

Beer Can Chicken is one of the first recipes my husband ever made for me. I think he was trying to impress me by balancing the chicken on the beer can as he headed out to the barbecue pit, but I was more impressed afterwards with the moistness of the chicken, rather than his balancing skills. We've made a couple of changes to "his" recipe as the years have gone by, but Beer Can Chicken remains one of the dishes with the best memories.

¼ cup mayonnaise

3 tablespoons dry rub seasoning (I use a BBQ blend)

1 (4-pound) whole chicken, neck and giblets removed, rinsed, and patted dry

2 tablespoons vegetable oil

1 (12-ounce) can beer

1) In a large bowl, combine mayonnaise with dry rub seasoning. Slather chicken, inside and out, with mixture, and refrigerate.

2) Set up your grill for indirect cooking. If using a charcoal grill, spread coals around outer edges, but not directly below food. On a gas grill, outer burners are lit, but not the middle one.

3) Open beer, and take several gulps, or discard some beer. Place on solid surface.

4) Grabbing a chicken leg in each hand, plop bird cavity over the beer can.

5) Transfer bird-on-a-can to your grill, in center of grate, over drip pan, balancing bird on its legs and the can like a tripod.

6) Cook over high indirect heat, with grill cover on, 1½–2 hours, or until temperature registers 180° on a meat thermometer inserted in thickest part of thigh.

7) Remove from grill; rest 10 minutes before carving. Be careful not to spill hot beer.

Cheesy Chicken Enchiladas

SERVES 4–6

2 pounds chicken, cubed

1 onion, chopped

2 tablespoons oil

1 (1¼-ounce) packet taco seasoning

1 (12-pack) 8-inch flour tortillas

1–2 (10-ounce) cans green chile enchilada sauce

1 pound shredded Mexican cheese blend

1) Sauté chicken and onion in oil in large skillet until chicken is cooked through. Remove from heat, and stir in taco seasoning to coat. Evenly divide mixture down middle of each tortilla, and roll up.

2) Place tortillas, flap down, in casserole dish. Pour enchilada sauce over tortillas, and top with cheese.

3) Bake at 350° for 15–20 minutes, or until cheese bubbles.

Repurpose-full

When shopping for recipe ingredients, consider brightly colored cans that can be repurposed into vases. Grocery store flowers become instantly festive when placed inside. Olé!

Southern Fried
Picnic Chicken

Southern Fried Picnic Chicken

SERVES 4–6

Have you ever been to a summertime picnic without fried chicken? Yeah, me neither. If we're being honest, I've always been terrified of frying chicken myself. It's generally easier to just purchase some, however, I'm pretty darn picky about the crispiness of the skin. When you make it yourself, you can control the ingredients and you can get the crispiness just the way your family likes it.

1 (2- to 3-pound) whole chicken, cut up

2 cups buttermilk

2 large eggs

2 cups all-purpose flour

2 tablespoons plus 2 teaspoons salt, divided

4 teaspoons black pepper, divided

1 tablespoon Creole seasoning

3 cups shortening

1) Rinse chicken with cold water; pat dry with paper towels, and set aside.

2) Whisk together milk and eggs in a bowl.

3) Combine flour, 2 tablespoons salt, 2 teaspoons black pepper, and Creole seasoning in a quart-size zip-top plastic freezer bag. Dip 2 chicken pieces in flour mixture, then into egg/milk mixture. Place chicken back into flour mixture in plastic bag; seal, and shake to coat. Remove chicken, and repeat with remaining pieces.

4) Melt shortening in a Dutch oven over medium heat to reach 350° on a thermometer. Fry chicken in batches 10 minutes on each side, or until cooked through and golden brown. Drain on paper towels. Sprinkle with remaining 2 teaspoons salt and 2 teaspoons black pepper.

Big Party Chicken & Sausage Jambalaya

SERVES 18–20

You'll be hard-pressed to find a large gathering around these parts that doesn't include jambalaya on the menu. Tailgates, family reunions, BBQs...if there's a crowd, there's typically jambalaya. And you don't need to be from the South to enjoy it either.

8 chicken bouillon cubes

13½ cups hot water

4 pounds smoked sausage, cut into ¾-inch slices

1 pound smoked tasso, cut into small pieces

1 tablespoon vegetable oil

4 pounds boneless, skinless chicken breasts, cubed

3 pounds onions, chopped

3 green bell peppers, chopped

1 head garlic, peeled, chopped

3 tablespoons salt

3½ teaspoons Creole seasoning

6 tablespoons Kitchen Bouquet

2 tablespoons Worcestershire

8 cups uncooked white rice

4 bunches green onions, chopped

1 bunch parsley, chopped

1) In a large saucepan, dissolve bouillon cubes in hot water.

2) Brown sausage and tasso in oil in 16-quart heavy pot. Remove with slotted spoon to paper towels to drain.

3) Add chicken to drippings in pot; cook until golden brown. Remove chicken to paper towels to drain.

4) Add onions, bell peppers, and garlic to drippings in pot; sauté until tender. Return sausage and chicken back to pot with vegetables. Cook 10 minutes.

5) Stir in dissolved bouillon, salt, Creole seasoning, Kitchen Bouquet, and Worcestershire. Bring to a boil.

6) Reduce heat to low; stir in rice. Cook, covered, 45 minutes, or until rice is tender. Stir in green onions and parsley. Cook, covered, 20–30 minutes longer.

Homemade Chili

SERVES 6

I rarely serve chili in a bowl anymore—I make Mason Jar Frito Pies instead. Layering it in a Mason jars with Fritos and all the fixin's is just so darn cute! And it's so easy to eat and clean up, whether you're tailgating or watching the game at home.

2 pounds lean ground beef

1 (46-ounce) can tomato juice

1 cup water

2 (6-ounce) cans tomato paste

1 (15-ounce) can kidney beans, drained

1 (15-ounce) can pinto beans, drained

½ tablespoon chili powder

1½ teaspoons cumin

½ teaspoon oregano

½ teaspoon white sugar

¼ teaspoon cayenne pepper

1 teaspoon black pepper

¼ cup chopped bell pepper

1½ cups chopped onions

MASON JAR FRITO PIES:

1 bag Fritos corn chips

1 cup shredded Cheddar cheese

½ cup sour cream

Jalapeño slices for garnish

1) Brown ground beef in a large pot over medium heat until cooked through; drain.

2) Add tomato juice, water, tomato paste, kidney beans, pinto beans, chili powder, cumin, oregano, sugar, cayenne pepper, black pepper, bell pepper, and chopped onions. Bring to a boil over medium-high heat.

3) Once chili starts to boil, lower heat, and simmer 2 hours, uncovered.

4) **Mason Jar Frito Pies:** Layer a handful of Fritos in each of 6 (12-ounce) Mason jars, and top with chili. Sprinkle with a couple tablespoons cheese, and add a big spoonful of sour cream. Garnish with a couple slices jalapeño.

Easy Cheesy Skillet Spaghetti

SERVES 4–6

1 pound ground beef

1 large onion, chopped

1 green bell pepper, chopped

7 ounces spaghetti, broken in half

½ (26-ounce) jar spaghetti sauce

¾ (14.5-ounce) container Campbell's Savory Portobello Mushroom Soup

¼ cup water

1 teaspoon dried oregano

1 teaspoon salt

1 teaspoon black pepper

1 cup shredded Italian blend cheese

1) In a large skillet or Dutch oven, cook beef and onion over medium heat until meat is no longer pink and onion is translucent.

2) Add bell pepper, uncooked spaghetti, spaghetti sauce, soup, water, oregano, salt and black pepper; bring to a boil.

3) Reduce heat, cover, and allow to simmer about 30 minutes or until spaghetti noodles are tender.

4) Sprinkle with cheese, cover, and heat until melted.

Bacon Cheeseburger Pie

SERVES 4–6

Good anytime, anywhere, for any age!

1 pound lean ground beef

1 onion, chopped

5 slices bacon, chopped

⅓ cup panko bread crumbs

1 teaspoon yellow mustard

3 tablespoons barbecue sauce

1 tablespoon ketchup

2 teaspoons Worcestershire

½ teaspoon black pepper

1 pie crust, uncooked (store bought or prepared)

2 cups shredded Cheddar cheese

¼ cup milk

1 egg

1) Preheat oven to 400°.

2) Brown ground beef, onion, and bacon in large skillet; drain well. Remove from heat, and stir in bread crumbs, mustard, barbecue sauce, ketchup, Worcestershire, and black pepper. Place mixture in pie crust.

3) In a small bowl, combine cheese, milk, and egg. Spread over meat mixture.

4) Cover edges of pie crust with foil or a pie shield to prevent overbrowning. Bake 15 minutes, remove foil, and bake an additional 15 minutes.

Pastalaya

Pastalaya

SERVES 8–10

Similar to jambalaya, Pastalaya is made of meat, vegetables, and starch. In this case, rather than rice, you'll use pasta, giving it the name Pastalaya. This recipe is less chunky and more creamy than jambalaya. The little grocery store near my home prepares Pastalaya on Wednesdays, and if you're not there prior to 12:30 p.m., you'll likely miss out on getting any that day.

1 pound pork, cubed

1 pound andouille/smoked sausage, sliced into ½-inch rounds

2 tablespoons butter

1 onion, chopped

2 stalks celery, chopped

1 green bell pepper, chopped

2 garlic cloves, minced

1 (10-ounce) can Rotel tomatoes, drained

1 cup chicken broth

¼ cup heavy cream

1 tablespoon Creole seasoning

1 teaspoon Tabasco

1 pound linguine pasta, cooked per package directions

2 green onions, chopped

Salt and black pepper to taste

1) In a large pot, brown pork and sausage in butter over medium-high heat. Remove from pot, and set aside.

2) Add onion, celery, and bell pepper to reserved drippings, and sauté until softened. Stir in garlic, Rotel tomatoes, chicken broth, cream, Creole seasoning, and Tabasco.

3) Return meat to pot, and bring to a boil.

4) Reduce heat, cover, and simmer on low 15–20 minutes, or until pork is cooked through.

5) Add cooked pasta and green onions; combine thoroughly. Season with salt and black pepper.

Old-Fashioned Pot Roast & Gravy

SERVES 4–6

1 (3-pound) boneless beef chuck roast

6 tablespoons all-purpose flour, divided

6 tablespoons butter, divided

1½ cups beef broth

1 medium onion, quartered

1 stalk celery, cut into pieces

1 teaspoon salt

½ teaspoon black pepper

4 carrots, cut into 2-inch chunks

1) Sprinkle roast with 1 tablespoon flour. In a Dutch oven, melt 3 tablespoons butter, and brown roast on all sides. Add broth, onion, celery, salt, and black pepper; bring to a boil. Reduce heat, cover, and simmer 1 hour.

2) Add carrots; cover, and simmer 45–60 minutes longer, or until meat is tender. Remove meat and carrots to a serving platter. Strain remaining juice, and set aside.

3) To make gravy, melt remaining 3 tablespoons butter in the same Dutch oven, and stir in remaining 5 tablespoons flour; cook and stir until bubbly.

4) Add 2 cups reserved roast juice, and blend until smooth. Cook and stir until thickened; add additional juice until gravy reaches desired consistency.

Low & Slow Garlic Bacon Pot Roast

SERVES 6–8

1 (3- to 3½-pound) beef chuck roast

Salt and black pepper to taste

2 tablespoons olive oil

6 slices applewood smoked bacon, diced

1½ cups chopped onion

8 garlic cloves, minced

1 (14½-ounce) can reduced-sodium beef broth

1 tablespoon thyme

1 tablespoon rosemary

3 medium carrots, cut into 2-inch pieces

10 small red potatoes, quartered

1) Preheat oven to 325°. Season meat with salt and black pepper. In a 6-quart Dutch oven, over medium-high heat, brown roast on all sides in hot oil. Remove to a plate.

2) Add bacon to Dutch oven, and cook until browned, stirring occasionally. Transfer half of cooked bacon to a paper towel-lined plate; cover until serving.

3) Add onion and garlic to Dutch oven; cook and stir 5 minutes, or until onion is tender and starting to brown. Return roast to Dutch oven.

4) Add broth, thyme, and rosemary; bring to a boil. Cover, and transfer to oven. Bake 1½ hours. Add carrots and potatoes. Bake, covered, for an additional 45 minutes or more, until meat and vegetables are tender.

5) Transfer beef and vegetables to a platter; cover, and keep warm. Skim fat from liquid; strain through a fine mesh sieve into a bowl; return to pot. Bring to a boil, reduce heat, and simmer 10–15 minutes. Serve with meat. When ready to serve, sprinkle reserved bacon over top.

Roasted Turkey with Bourbon Gravy

SERVES 10–12

(Adapted from the Baton Rouge Junior League's Warm Welcomes) Before I got married, I never once considered making my own turkey. I somehow assumed there would always be someone around to prepare the turkey while I contributed a side dish. That was until I married my husband who truly enjoys preparing the big bird! Consider this your failproof turkey recipe as you ease yourself into the world of roasting.

1 (17-pound) turkey

1 onion, chopped

1 stalk celery, chopped

2 Granny Smith apples, chopped

1 tablespoon poultry seasoning

1 stick butter, melted

1½ tablespoons salt

1½ tablespoons black pepper

BOURBON GRAVY:

3 cups water

½ cup all-purpose flour

¼ cup bourbon

1) Place oven rack in bottom ⅔ of oven, and preheat oven to 350°. Remove neck and giblet bag from turkey. Rinse turkey, and pat dry.

2) Combine onion, celery, apples, and poultry seasoning in a bowl; stuff turkey with the mixture. Brush outside of turkey with melted butter, then sprinkle with salt and black pepper. Place turkey, neck, and giblets in roasting pan.

3) Bake about 4 hours. Turkey is done when a meat thermometer registers 180°. Remove turkey to a platter to carve, discard neck and giblets, and reserve pan drippings for gravy.

4) **Bourbon Gravy:** Add water to pan drippings, and stir to loosen the browned bits. Pour into a saucepan, and bring to a simmer.

5) Mix flour and bourbon in a bowl, then whisk into drippings. Cook over medium-high heat 10 minutes, or until thickened to a gravy consistency.

Honey Baked Ham

SERVES 8–10

1 whole (5- to 10-pound) precooked, spiral cut ham

1 stick butter

½ cup brown sugar

¼ cup honey

⅛ cup orange juice

¼ teaspoon ground cinnamon

¼ teaspoon ground cloves

1) Preheat oven to 325°.

2) Line a pan large enough to hold ham and its juices with a few layers of heavy-duty aluminum foil, or use disposable roasting pans for easy cleanup.

3) Combine butter, brown sugar, honey, orange juice, and spices in a heavy saucepan. Heat on low until butter is melted, and ingredients are evenly mixed.

4) Place ham in lined pan, and brush with the warm honey glaze.

5) Bake 1–1½ hours, depending on size of ham. (Check packaging for exact cooking times.) Every 15 minutes or so, brush on remaining glaze.

6) If you'd like the top of ham more golden brown, turn on broiler for a minute to caramelize the top. You can also add additional glaze with some extra brown sugar, and use a kitchen blow torch.

7) Let ham rest 10–15 minutes, then remove to a platter to serve.

Soups & Salads

Watermelon Centerpiece

Don't toss the watermelon rind! Cut a thin slice off bottom of "vase" so it will stand up. Sit watermelon upright and use a serrated knife to cut off the top of your watermelon, then run a cut along the inside. Scoop out watermelon and use it in Watermelon Mojito Salad (page 145). Arrange with flowers and use as your centerpiece.

Tomato Basil Soup with Grilled Cheese Bites

SERVES 8

2 (14-ounce) cans diced tomatoes, undrained

1 cup finely diced onions

1 cup finely diced celery

2 tablespoons tomato paste

4 cups chicken broth

1 teaspoon oregano

¼ cup fresh basil

1 stick butter

½ cup all-purpose flour

1 cup grated Parmesan cheese

1½ cups half-and-half

Salt and black pepper to taste

1) Add diced tomatoes, onion, celery, tomato paste, chicken broth, oregano, and basil to slow cooker. Cover, and cook on LOW 5–6 hours.

2) About 30 minutes before soup is ready, prepare a roux by melting butter in a skillet over medium-low heat, then whisking in flour. Whisk constantly for about 10 minutes or until roux turns golden brown. Slowly add 1 cup soup from slow cooker. Whisk together until smooth, then add roux mixture back into slow cooker; stir to combine well.

3) Add Parmesan cheese, half-and-half, salt and black pepper; stir to combine well. Cover, and cook on LOW an additional 30 minutes.

4) Pour soup into blender to get out all the clumps and purée until smooth (you may need to do this in batches, depending on size of your blender).

5) Serve with your favorite grilled cheese sandwich recipe, bread ends removed, and sliced finger sandwich style.

Crawfish Chowder

SERVES 8–10

I often go back and forth between calling this recipe a chowder and a bisque. It's sort of both. While traditionally bisques are smooth and creamy and chowders are chunky, this recipe is a bit of both. Feel free to call it whatever you'd like, and if you're still torn just call it a chowder-bisque.

2 bundles green onions, chopped

1 cup chopped mushrooms

1½ sticks butter, divided

2 pounds frozen crawfish tails, thawed

½ teaspoon cayenne pepper

1 tablespoon Tabasco

2 (10¾-ounce) cans cream of potato soup

2 (10¾-ounce) cans cream of mushroom soup

1 (15¼-ounce) can whole-kernel corn, drained

2 cups half-and-half

2 (8-ounce) packages cream cheese, cubed

1) In a skillet, sauté green onions and mushrooms in ¾ stick butter until soft.

2) Add crawfish tails and remaining ¾ stick butter; sauté until crawfish is heated through. Stir in cayenne pepper and Tabasco; cook 5 minutes.

3) In another pot, combine soups and corn, and heat on medium low. Keep stirring, and slowly add half-and-half and cream cheese. When cream cheese has melted, add crawfish mixture. Reduce heat to low, and simmer 15–20 minutes.

A Bit of Everything Gumbo

A Bit of Everything Gumbo

SERVES 6–8

½ cup peanut oil

½ cup all-purpose flour

1 green bell pepper, chopped

1 medium onion, chopped

3 celery stalks, chopped

4 garlic cloves, chopped

1 tablespoon Creole seasoning

4 cups chicken broth

1 tablespoon Worcestershire

12 ounces smoked andouille sausage, sliced into ¼-inch rounds

1½ pounds chicken breasts, cubed

1 teaspoon salt

1 teaspoon black pepper

½ teaspoon cayenne

2 pounds shrimp, peeled and deveined

8 cups freshly cooked white rice

1 bunch green onions, chopped, for garnish

1) Make a roux by heating oil in large, heavy pot or Dutch oven over medium heat for about 2 minutes. Sprinkle flour over hot oil, and whisk until smooth. Cook, stirring constantly with a wooden spoon, until roux is the color of peanut butter, about 15 minutes. Reduce heat to low, and continue cooking and stirring until roux is the color of milk chocolate—not dark chocolate, though!

2) Add bell pepper, onion, and celery. Cook until tender, stirring often, about 5 minutes. Add garlic and Creole seasoning. Whisking constantly, add broth. Stir in Worcestershire, and simmer 30 minutes.

3) In medium-size skillet, brown sausage; drain on paper towels. In same skillet, cook chicken until done.

4) Add sausage and chicken to large pot, and simmer 10 minutes. Season with salt, black pepper, and cayenne. Add shrimp, and simmer just until shrimp are lightly pink, about 5 minutes.

5) Serve over a scoop of hot rice, and top with green onions.

Creamy Shrimp & Corn Soup

SERVES 6–8

There's a little café where I grew up in central Louisiana that serves the most delicious Shrimp & Corn Soup. It is so good that even if you're not in the mood for soup as a meal that day, you still order a cup as an appetizer because you know you'll regret it if you don't! I re-created that beloved soup for those days when I'm craving the flavors of home.

½ cup chopped onion

2 tablespoon chopped celery

1 stick plus 2 tablespoons butter, divided

¼ cup all-purpose flour

1 cup chicken broth

1½ cups heavy whipping cream

1 (15-ounce) can cream-style corn

1 cup frozen corn

1 pound shrimp, peeled and deveined

2 teaspoons Creole seasoning, divided

¼ cup chopped green onions

¼ cup sherry

1½ teaspoons salt

1) Sauté onion and celery in 1 stick butter in a medium saucepan 3 minutes, or until onion is translucent.

2) Add flour, and mix well. Cook 3–5 minutes, stirring constantly. Gradually add broth, stirring constantly to prevent burning. Stir in cream and corn. Cook over medium-low heat 10 minutes, stirring frequently.

3) In a separate pan, combine shrimp, remaining 2 tablespoons butter, and 1 teaspoon Creole seasoning; sauté until shrimp turn pink, 3–5 minutes.

4) Fold shrimp and green onions into corn mixture. Stir in sherry, salt, and remaining 1 teaspoon Creole seasoning. Simmer just until heated through, and ladle into soup bowls.

Grilled Chicken Sensation Salad

SERVES 6–8

SENSATION SALAD DRESSING:

½ cup vegetable oil

½ cup olive oil

2 tablespoons lemon juice

2 tablespoons white vinegar

3 garlic cloves, minced, mashed

Salt and black pepper to taste

SALAD:

4 boneless, skinless chicken breasts

1 small head ice-cold iceberg lettuce, torn into bite-size pieces

2 tablespoons chopped fresh parsley

1 cup grated Romano cheese

1) **Sensation Salad Dressing:** In a 1-quart container with a lid, blend together oils, lemon juice, vinegar, garlic, salt, and black pepper. Cover, and shake vigorously to mix. Refrigerate 24 hours for flavors to incorporate. Shake dressing well before serving.

2) **Salad:** Moisten a paper towel with cooking oil, and using long-handled tongs, lightly coat grill rack. Grill chicken, covered, over medium heat, or broil 4 inches from heat 4–7 minutes on each side, or until a meat thermometer reads 170°.

3) Remove chicken to a cutting board, and when cool enough to handle, slice chicken against the grain crosswise into ½-inch slices.

4) Wash lettuce; dry, and tear into bite-size pieces. Refrigerate until ready to use.

5) Place torn lettuce and parsley in a large mixing bowl, top with Salad Dressing, and toss to coat well. Add Romano cheese, and toss gently. Top with sliced chicken.

Mason Jar Green Goddess Salad

SERVES 8

Mason jars and picnic parties go together like peanut butter and jelly! Functional for predetermined serving sizes as well as vessels for consumption, it doesn't really get any easier than picnicking with the Mason jar. Use them for salads, for beverages, for holding utensils...the options are limitless.

1 medium head iceberg lettuce

1 tablespoon salt

8 ounces fresh green beans, stems trimmed

8 ounces pasta, cooked al dente, drained

2 chicken breasts, grilled (I used precooked Tyson's chicken, heated through)

4 hard-boiled eggs, peeled, chopped

2 small ripe tomatoes, cored and chopped, if desired

¼ cup niçoise olives

Salt and freshly ground black pepper

1) Wash lettuce leaves, dry, then tear into bite-size pieces; set aside.

2) In a medium saucepan, bring 3–4 cups water to boil; add 1 tablespoon salt and green beans. Cook until tender but crisp, 3–5 minutes. Drain beans, transfer to a bowl of ice water, and let stand until just cool, about 30 seconds; dry beans well. Set aside.

3) Chop chicken and eggs separately.

4) Layer into 8 Mason jars, beginning with lettuce, then pasta, beans, chicken, eggs, tomatoes, and olives. Do not add dressing. Cover and place in refrigerator until ready to eat. Pour contents onto a plate or bowl, and add dressing of your choice.

Creamy Homemade Coleslaw

SERVES 8

1 cup mayonnaise

2–3 tablespoons fresh lemon juice

2 tablespoons sugar

1 teaspoon salt

6 cups shredded cabbage (1 small head yields about 8 cups)

1 cup shredded carrots

½ cup chopped or thinly sliced green bell pepper

1) In a large bowl, combine mayonnaise, lemon juice, sugar, and salt.

2) Add cabbage, carrots, and bell pepper; toss to coat well. Cover, and chill until ready to serve.

Cucumber & Onion Salad

SERVES 4–6

3 English cucumbers

½ medium-size Vidalia onion

½ cup white vinegar

½ cup water

1 garlic clove, finely minced

2 teaspoons sugar

1 teaspoon salt

Black pepper to taste

1) Peel cucumbers, and thinly slice. Peel onion, and thinly slice. Combine cucumbers and onion in a large bowl.

2) In a separate bowl, combine remaining ingredients, and pour over cucumbers and onion. Refrigerate at least an hour before serving.

Grandma's Family Reunion
Potato Salad

Grandma's Family Reunion Potato Salad

SERVES 8

Grandma made this potato salad for every family reunion, and now I make it to carry on the tradition—reunions wouldn't be the same without it, and it brings back such fond memories. Every family seems to have their own way of making potato salad. We like ours with spicy brown mustard and a little relish.

4 pounds red potatoes (about 8)

3 hard-boiled eggs, chopped

¾ cup mayonnaise

1½ teaspoons sweet pickle relish

1 tablespoon spicy brown mustard

1½ teaspoons salt

¾ teaspoon black pepper

1 green onion, chopped, for garnish

Paprika for garnish

1) In a large stockpot, cook potatoes in boiling water 40 minutes or until tender; drain, and cool.

2) Peel potatoes, and cut into 1-inch cubes. Add eggs, and mix.

3) Stir together mayonnaise, relish, mustard, salt, and black pepper; gently stir into potato mixture.

4) Garnish with green onion and a sprinkle of paprika.

5) Serve immediately, or cover and chill until ready to serve.

Easy Waldorf Salad

SERVES ?

An incredibly easy way to enjoy the famed Waldorf-Astoria Hotel salad right in the comfort of your own home or even a picnic blanket in the park, the Easy Waldorf Salad is one of my favorites. Something about it just says lovely lunch companion! It's light and refreshing, and you can add or take away ingredients to your preference. Use pecans rather than walnuts, add a bit of celery, and omit the raisins if you don't like them. It travels well, too. Just keep the salad in a sealed container and lettuce leaves in a Ziploc bag. Keep it all cold in a cooler, and assemble it once you arrive at your destination.

½ cup walnut halves

½ cup nonfat yogurt

2 tablespoons light mayonnaise

1 teaspoon honey

¼ teaspoon cinnamon, plus a little extra for garnish

1 lemon, halved

Black pepper to taste

2 large Gala apples

20 grapes, halved

¼ cup raisins

Lettuce leaves for garnish

1) Preheat oven to 350°. Spread walnuts on a baking sheet, and bake about 10 minutes. Allow to cool, then break into small pieces.

2) Whisk yogurt, mayonnaise, honey, cinnamon, and juice of ½ lemon in a large bowl, and season with black pepper.

3) Halve, core, and cut apples into cubes, leaving skin intact. Combine apples, grapes, and raisins in a bowl, sprinkle with juice from remaining ½ lemon, then toss with yogurt mixture. Cover, and refrigerate.

4) When ready to serve, toss walnuts onto the salad. Arrange lettuce leaves, and place salad on top to serve.

Watermelon Mojito Salad

SERVES 8

The combination of watermelon and cucumber is sort of an odd one, but both provide intense hydration. Light, refreshing, and a little bit tangy, serve this salad in the heat of summer, or as a poolside snack, and watch them keep coming back.

6 cups cubed seedless watermelon

2 medium English cucumbers, halved, sliced

3 tablespoons finely chopped fresh mint

½ cup fresh lime juice (about 4 limes)

2 tablespoons extra virgin olive oil

½ teaspoon sea salt

¼ teaspoon black pepper

1) Combine watermelon, cucumber, and mint in a large bowl.

2) In separate bowl, whisk remaining ingredients together. Pour over salad, tossing to coat.

Chicken Salad Croissants

SERVES 8–10

A classic picnic staple, chicken salad gets an upgrade by being served on croissants rather than bread. The croissants hold their shape in the refrigerator a little better, allowing them to be prepared ahead of time. Get creative with additions, and consider adding sliced grapes or slivered almonds. I like to add pecans, but the nuts are entirely optional.

6 cups chopped cooked chicken

1¼ cups mayonnaise

3 green onions, thinly sliced

3 stalks celery, diced

2 teaspoons lemon juice

¼ teaspoon garlic powder

1 teaspoon dill weed

⅓ cup grated Parmesan cheese

Salt and black pepper to taste

¼ cup chopped pecans (optional)

8–10 large croissants, split in half lengthwise

1) Stir together chicken and next 7 ingredients; salt and black pepper to taste. Sprinkle in chopped pecans, if desired.

2) Spoon mixture over croissant bottoms; replace tops. Serve immediately, or cover and refrigerate until ready to serve.

The Very Best Egg Salad Croissants

SERVES 4

6 hard-boiled eggs, peeled and chopped

¼ cup mayonnaise, plus more for spreading

½ teaspoon Dijon mustard

½ tablespoon dill pickle relish

½ tablespoon sweet pickle relish

½ teaspoon onion powder

Salt and black pepper to taste

¼ cup thinly sliced pimento-stuffed olives

4 romaine lettuce leaves

4 large croissants, split in half

Paprika (optional)

1) Combine eggs with next 6 ingredients; mix well. Stir in olives.

2) Place lettuce over bottom halves of croissants; top with egg mixture, and sprinkle with paprika, if desired. Add croissant tops.

Cool it!

If you are serving salads or dressings with mayonnaise or eggs, pack them in an ice chest, and keep chilled until ready to serve. And remember to return them to the cooler as soon as possible after eating. If you plan to grill raw meat or poultry at your picnic, package it separately and away from other foods in the ice chest—or better yet, store in a separate cooler.

Vegetables & Sides

Smooth Sailing

Sail away with these Sweet Potato "Boats." Simply tie a piece of remnant fabric or ribbon to a cocktail stirrer that has been cut down for a clever sail for your boat. Imagine how cute these would be at a nautical-inspired gathering!

Creole-Style String Beans

SERVES 6

My grandmother called them string beans, but the tough string was bred out of green beans years ago, making that title not as appropriate. Whether you call them string beans, green beans, snap beans, bush beans, or pole beans, these are absolutely delicious!

5 strips bacon, cut in pieces

1 green bell pepper, finely chopped

1 medium onion, finely chopped

1 (14½-ounce) can diced tomatoes, drained

2 (14½-ounce) cans cut green beans

1 teaspoon Worcestershire

¼ cup mayonnaise

½ teaspoon salt

Dash of black pepper

Dash of cayenne

1 (8-ounce) can sliced mushrooms

½ cup bread crumbs

3 tablespoons butter

1) Preheat oven to 350°.

2) Cook bacon, bell pepper, and onion in cast-iron skillet 5–8 minutes. Drain.

3) Add tomatoes, and simmer 5 minutes. Stir in beans, Worcestershire, mayonnaise, and seasonings; blend thoroughly. Add mushrooms.

4) Cover with bread crumbs, dot with butter, and bake, uncovered, 20 minutes.

Sautéed Green Beans with Pecans

SERVES 8–10

¼ cup olive oil

1 small onion, sliced

1 (2-pound) bag frozen cut green beans, thawed

2 teaspoons sugar

1 teaspoon salt

½ teaspoon black pepper

⅓ cup teriyaki sauce

3 tablespoons butter

1 cup chopped pecans

1) Warm sauté pan on medium-high heat. Add olive oil, and sauté onion until tender.

2) Add beans, and cook, stirring constantly, until beans begin to lightly brown.

3) Add sugar, salt, black pepper, and teriyaki sauce, and continue to cook an additional 2 minutes.

4) Add butter. When butter has melted, stir in pecans. Cook, stirring constantly 2–3 more minutes.

Prosciutto Wrapped Asparagus

SERVES 4

6 ounces sliced prosciutto, halved horizontally

1 pound asparagus, trimmed

1 tablespoon olive oil

1) Wrap a halved prosciutto slice onto each asparagus spear at an angle, covering entire length of the spear.

2) Heat olive oil in a large skillet over medium-high heat. Add wrapped asparagus, and cook until prosciutto is crisp and asparagus is tender, 2–3 minutes.

Impossibly Easy
Corn Pudding

Impossibly Easy Corn Pudding

SERVES 6–8

1 (10-ounce) can whole-kernel corn, drained

1 (10-ounce) can cream-style corn

1 stick butter, softened

1 (8-ounce) container sour cream

1 (8-ounce) box Jiffy corn muffin mix

1) Preheat oven to 350°.

2) In a medium-size bowl, mix together corn, butter, and sour cream. Add corn muffin mix, and stir until well combined.

3) Pour into casserole dish. Bake 45 minutes, or until no longer wiggly.

Zesty Mexican Street Corn

SERVES 4

4 ears corn

½ cup mayonnaise

1½ cups sour cream

¼ cup chopped fresh cilantro

1 lime, plus more for garnish

1 cup freshly grated Parmesan

Chili powder to taste

1) Remove corn husks, leaving core attached. Grill corn, turning once, on a hot grill (or in oven in cast-iron skillet) until slightly charred.

2) In a small bowl, mix mayonnaise, sour cream, and cilantro.

3) Remove corn from grill, and slather with mayonnaise mixture. Squeeze juice from lime juice over corn, and sprinkle heavily with Parmesan and chili powder.

4) Serve with additional lime wedges.

Honey Bourbon Baked Beans

SERVES 8

When Julie Murphy-Jones sent me her Nana Murphy's recipe, and described it as "the world's best baked beans"—well, I just had to try them for myself. I loved her recipe, but couldn't resist putting my own spin on it with honey and a bit of brown sugar. I'd love to see what Nana Murphy would think of my interpretation—I believe she would approve.

4 slices bacon

1 small onion, diced

2 (16-ounce) cans pork and beans

½ cup honey bourbon whiskey

⅓ cup honey barbecue sauce

⅓ cup dark brown sugar

⅓ cup molasses

½ teaspoon dry mustard

1) Cook bacon in a frying pan over medium heat until crisp. Remove bacon, and drain on paper towels. Crumble bacon once cooled.

2) Keep 2–3 tablespoons bacon drippings in pan. Sauté onion in drippings over high heat until tender and translucent.

3) In a greased baking dish, combine bacon and onion together with remaining ingredients. Bake, uncovered, at 375° for 1 hour or until sauce has thickened.

Sweet Potato "Boats"

SERVES 5–6

For special celebrations, birthdays, and holidays, my mother would always prepare Sweet Potato "Boats." I can't tell you how much I look forward to seeing the sweet potatoes in their skins, affectionately referred to simply as "boats" in our family. They are very similar to twice-baked potatoes, but in sweet potato form. And just like my Sweet Potato Casserole (page 82), they hold nothing back with their marshmallow and candied topping.

3 large sweet potatoes

4 tablespoons packed light brown sugar

3 tablespoons butter, melted

Pinch of salt

1 teaspoon cinnamon

TOPPING:

3 tablespoons all-purpose flour

¼ teaspoon cinnamon

¼ cup chopped walnuts

2 tablespoons butter

3 tablespoons packed brown sugar

½ cup miniature marshmallows

1) Prick sweet potatoes with a fork or knife, and bake at 350° for 30 minutes or until soft. When cool enough to handle, slice potatoes in half, and scoop out centers into a bowl, leaving ¼-inch border of sweet potato skin intact.

2) Combine potato meal, brown sugar, butter, salt, and cinnamon until smooth. Spoon mixture back into sweet potato shells.

3) **Topping:** In small bowl, mix together Topping ingredients until butter starts to warm, and ingredients start holding together.

4) Top filled sweet potatoes with Topping, and bake at 350° for 20–30 minutes.

5) Remove from oven, and top each potato with mini marshmallows.

6) Return to oven, and bake until marshmallows are golden brown, 3–5 minutes, or on broil for 1–2 minutes, watching closely so they don't burn.

Baked Mac & Cheese Muffins

MAKES 8 MUFFINS

When contributing to a picnic, potluck, or porch party, you want dishes that are both incredibly delicious and easy to transport, as well being easy to eat. These Baked Mac & Cheese Muffins hit all the marks.

1½ cups crushed Ritz butter crackers (about 35)

2 cups grated Cheddar cheese, divided

4 tablespoons unsalted butter, melted

½ (16-ounce) package elbow macaroni, cooked, drained

2 large eggs, beaten

½ cup milk

¼ cup sour cream

2 tablespoons cold unsalted butter, cut into small cubes

¼ teaspoon salt

¼ teaspoon black pepper

1) Preheat oven to 350°. Lightly grease 8 cups of a 12-cup muffin pan.

2) In a bowl, combine crushed crackers, 1 cup Cheddar cheese, and melted butter. Divide mixture among prepared muffin cups, and press firmly into bottom and up sides.

3) In a large bowl, mix cooked macaroni with ½ cup Cheddar cheese.

4) In a separate bowl, combine eggs, milk, sour cream, 2 tablespoons cold butter pieces, salt and black pepper. Stir into macaroni mixture.

5) Spoon 2 tablespoons macaroni mixture into each muffin cup filled with cracker mixture, and evenly top with remaining ½ cup Cheddar cheese. Bake until cheese is browned and slightly crispy, about 25 minutes. Allow muffins to cool slightly before removing. Serve warm.

Okra & Corn Maque Choux

SERVES 6–8

4 ears fresh corn

½ pound bacon

2 tablespoons butter

1 yellow onion, chopped

1 tablespoon minced garlic

1 tablespoon Creole seasoning

2 pounds sliced okra

½ teaspoon thyme

2 bay leaves

Salt and black pepper to taste

1 cup chicken broth

2 small tomatoes, chopped

1) Scrape kernels from corn cobs, saving as much pulp and milk as possible; set aside.

2) Fry bacon in a 3-quart Dutch oven over medium heat. When crisp, remove, and drain on a paper-towel-lined plate. Reserve bacon fat in pan.

3) Add butter and onion to Dutch oven, and sauté 5 minutes. Add garlic, and cook another minute.

4) Increase heat to medium-high; add Creole seasoning, okra, thyme, and bay leaves. Add salt and black pepper as needed. Cook, stirring occasionally, about 5 minutes.

5) Add corn; cook, stirring occasionally, 2–3 minutes. Add broth, and cook 5 more minutes, or until mixture begins to thicken.

6) Toss in chopped tomatoes, and cook just until tomatoes are heated through. Crumble bacon, add to vegetables, and simmer an additional 5 minutes.

Spinach Madeleine Remix

Spinach Madeleine Remix

SERVES 6

One of the most beloved recipes from the Baton Rouge Junior League's *River Road Recipes* is Spinach Madeleine. A unique blend of creamy spinach and spicy cheese, this dish has made its way onto South Louisiana holiday tables for decades. The original recipe, published in 1959, called for using a jalapeño cheese roll that has been discontinued—much to the dismay of the entire state of Louisiana. I've seen it "remixed" a multitude of ways, from Chef John Folse to Kay Robertson (Duck Dynasty), and as so many have done before, I have remixed it myself as well.

1 (1-pound) package frozen chopped spinach

2 tablespoons butter

1 tablespoon flour

2 tablespoons chopped onion

¾ cup Swanson Cream Starter

½ cup reserved spinach liquor

½ teaspoon black pepper

½ teaspoon garlic salt

½ teaspoon Creole seasoning

Salt to taste

6 ounces jalapeño Cheddar cheese with red peppers, cut into small cubes

1 teaspoon Worcestershire

Flavored bread crumbs (optional)

1) Cook spinach according to package directions. Drain, reserving excess liquid.

2) Melt butter in saucepan over low heat. Add flour, stirring until blended and smooth, but not brown. Slowly add reserved spinach liquid, stirring constantly to avoid lumps. Cook, stirring, until smooth and thick.

3) Add black pepper, garlic salt, Creole seasoning, salt, and cheese cubes; stir until cheese is melted. Mix in Worcestershire.

4) Combine cheese mixture with cooked spinach; serve immediately.

Make Ahead:

Place combined mixture in casserole dish, and top with flavored bread crumbs. Refrigerate overnight. Bake at 350° for 30 minutes, or until bubbly. (The flavor is intensified if kept in refrigerator overnight.)

Buttermilk Crust Green Tomato Pie

SERVES 6–8

BUTTERMILK CRUST:

2½ cups all-purpose flour

2 teaspoons salt

2 teaspoons sugar

1 cup cold unsalted butter

6–8 tablespoons buttermilk

FILLING:

¼ cup diced Vidalia onion

½ teaspoon salt

¼ teaspoon black pepper

1 teaspoon chopped fresh basil

½ teaspoon dried oregano

3–4 green tomatoes, peeled and sliced

¼ cup mayonnaise

1 cup grated Cheddar cheese

1) **Buttermilk Crust:** Combine flour, salt, and sugar in a medium bowl. Using a pastry blender, cut in cubed butter until it resembles coarse crumbs. Gradually add buttermilk until dough ball comes together. Turn out onto lightly floured surface.

2) Divide in half; shape into 2 disks. Cover with plastic wrap, and refrigerate at least 30 minutes.

3) Preheat oven to 400°. On lightly floured surface, roll one disc of dough to cover 9-inch pie plate. Bake 5–7 minutes, or until lightly golden.

4) **Filling:** Reduce oven temperature to 375°. In medium bowl, combine onion, salt, black pepper, basil, and oregano.

5) Layer tomatoes in baked pie crust, and top with onion mixture.

6) Combine mayonnaise and cheese, and spread evenly over tomatoes, extending to edges.

7) Roll out second disc of dough, and cover top of pie, crimping edges. Cut a few slits for venting. Bake 30–35 minutes.

New Orleans-Style Oyster Dressing

SERVES 10–12

1 loaf stale French bread, cut into small cubes

1 pint oysters (reserve oyster liquor)

1 stick plus 2 tablespoons butter, divided

1 onion, chopped

1 bunch green onions, chopped

1 large green bell pepper, chopped

2 garlic cloves, minced

1 egg, beaten

1 bunch parsley, trimmed and chopped

Salt and black pepper to taste

¼ cup Italian bread crumbs

1) Preheat oven to 200°. Place bread cubes on a cookie sheet, and dry in oven 5–8 minutes. Set aside in large bowl.

2) Drain oysters over a bowl, reserving liquor. Chop oysters, and set aside.

3) Measure oyster liquor, and add enough chicken broth or water to measure 1 cup. Pour over bread cubes to soak.

4) In large skillet, melt 1 stick butter over medium heat. Add onion, green onions, bell pepper, and garlic. Cook, stirring frequently, until tender. Add chopped oysters, soaked bread cubes, and oyster liquor, and cook until oysters are heated through, about 3 minutes.

5) Remove from heat; stir in egg and parsley. Season to taste with salt and black pepper.

6) Spoon dressing into buttered 2-quart baking dish, and sprinkle with bread crumbs. Cover with aluminum foil, and bake at 350° for 20 minutes.

7) Remove foil, and bake an additional 5–10 minutes, or until top is bubbly and golden brown.

Cookies & Candies

Set Up a To-Go Station for Leftovers

Chances are you'll have lots of leftovers following your potluck. Rather than tossing the food or allowing it to go to waste, consider preparing a packaging station for those leftovers with disposable containers, twine, and labels so that guests go home with lunch for the next day, or goodies for their sweet tooth.

White Chocolate Gingerbread

White Chocolate Gingerbread Cookies

MAKES 3 DOZEN COOKIES

2 sticks butter, softened

1 cup sugar

¼ cup water

1½ teaspoons baking soda

¾ cup molasses

4½ cups all-purpose flour

¼ teaspoon salt

1½ tablespoons ground ginger

½ teaspoon ground allspice

½ teaspoon ground cinnamon

12 ounces white chocolate chips

1 tablespoon vegetable oil

1) Beat butter and sugar together with electric mixer on medium speed until light and fluffy.

2) In a separate bowl, stir together water and baking soda until dissolved, then add molasses.

3) Combine flour, salt, and spices in a large bowl, then slowly add to butter mixture alternately with molasses mixture. Shape mixture into a ball and cover with plastic wrap. Chill at least 1 hour.

4) Preheat oven to 350°. On lightly floured surface, roll out dough ball to about ¼-inch thickness. Use a cookie cutter to cut desired shape, and place onto parchment-lined baking sheets about 2 inches apart.

5) Bake 12–15 minutes. Allow to cool completely on a wire rack.

6) Once completely cooled, heat white chocolate in microwave with vegetable oil; mix thoroughly. Dip each cookie halfway into white chocolate, and allow to set for a couple of hours, or pop into refrigerator for 30 minutes.

Chocolate Chunk Cookies

MAKES 6–7 DOZEN

Hands down the best chocolate chip cookie on the block, but don't just take my word for it. Try them out for yourself!

2 sticks butter, softened

1½ cups firmly packed brown sugar

2 teaspoons vanilla extract

1 teaspoon baking soda

¼ teaspoon salt

3 large eggs

2¼ cups all-purpose flour

2½ cups semisweet chocolate chips

1 cup coarsely chopped walnuts

1) Preheat oven to 400°.

2) Beat butter, brown sugar, vanilla extract, baking soda, and salt with electric mixer on medium until creamy. Beat in eggs until fluffy.

3) With mixer on low speed, add flour, a little at a time, until blended. Fold in chocolate chips and walnuts.

4) Using a cookie scoop, drop onto ungreased cookie sheet approximately 2 inches apart. Bake 8 minutes or until golden.

5) Cool on cookie sheet 2 minutes before removing to a wire rack to cool completely.

Minty Triple Chocolate Cookies

MAKES 5–6 DOZEN

1½ sticks butter, softened

1 cup sugar

1 egg

1¾ cups all-purpose flour

½ cup cocoa

¼ teaspoon salt

¼ teaspoon baking soda

3 ounces semisweet chocolate, chopped

1 teaspoon canola oil

1 (10-ounce) package Andes Crème de Menthe Baking Chips

1) Preheat oven to 350°. In a small bowl, cream butter and sugar until light and fluffy, then beat in egg.

2) In another bowl, whisk together flour, cocoa, salt, and baking soda. Gradually add to creamed mixture.

3) Shape dough into 1-inch balls, and place on ungreased baking sheets.

4) Flatten slightly, and bake 6–8 minutes or until set.

5) Cool in pan about 5 minutes, then place on wire racks to cool completely.

6) Meanwhile, melt semisweet chocolate and oil in microwave until smooth.

7) Drizzle over cookies, and sprinkle Andes mint chips in center of each cookie while chocolate is still wet.

8) Let stand until chocolate sets.

Bakery-Style Sugar Cookies

MAKES 14 OVERSIZED COOKIES

2 sticks unsalted butter, softened

1½ cups sugar

½ cup packed brown sugar

2 eggs

1½ teaspoons grated lemon peel

2 tablespoons lemon juice

3 cups all-purpose flour

1 teaspoon baking soda

¼ teaspoon salt

¼ teaspoon cream of tartar

4 teaspoons coarse sugar

1) Preheat oven to 350°.

2) In a large bowl, cream butter and sugars until light and fluffy. Beat in eggs. Beat in lemon peel and juice.

3) In another bowl, whisk flour, baking soda, salt, and cream of tartar; gradually beat into creamed mixture.

4) Shape ¼ cupfuls of dough into balls. Place 6 inches apart on greased baking sheets. Flatten to ¾-inch thickness with bottom of a measuring cup. Lightly brush tops with water; sprinkle with coarse sugar.

5) Bake 12–15 minutes, or until light brown. Remove from pans to wire racks to cool completely. Store in airtight containers.

Butter Toffee Crunch Cookies

MAKES 3–4 DOZEN COOKIES

3 cups all-purpose flour

1 teaspoon salt

1 teaspoon baking soda

3 sticks butter, softened

1¼ cups sugar

¾ cup packed brown sugar

1½ teaspoons vanilla extract

2 eggs

1½ cups butter toffee peanuts

1) Mix flour, salt, and baking soda together in a small bowl.

2) Beat butter, sugar, brown sugar, and vanilla in a mixing bowl until light and fluffy, scraping the bowl occasionally. Add eggs, 1 at a time, beating well after each addition. Add flour mixture gradually, beating until a soft dough forms. Stir in peanuts.

3) Drop by rounded teaspoonfuls onto parchment-lined cookie sheets. Bake at 325° for 12–15 minutes, or until light brown. Cool on cookie sheet 2 minutes, then remove to a wire rack to cool completely. Store in airtight container.

Pecan Praline King Cake Cookies

SERVES 12–15

The marriage of Louisiana's beloved king cake and pecan pralines all wrapped up in a bite-size explosion of happiness. This is the prize-winning recipe I created for the 2013 Dixie Crystals Cookie Bake-Off championship!

1 cup butter, softened

1¾ cups sugar, divided

2 tablespoons ground cinnamon, divided

3 egg yolks

1 tablespoon honey

1 teaspoon vanilla extract

½ teaspoon lemon extract

2½ cups all-purpose flour

1 teaspoon baking powder

½ teaspoon salt

½ teaspoon cream of tartar

PECAN PRALINE TOPPING:

1 cup sugar

1 cup brown sugar

½ cup evaporated milk

2 tablespoons butter

1¼ cups pecan halves

¼ teaspoon vanilla extract

Purple, green, and gold sprinkles and edible glitter for garnish (optional)

1) Preheat oven to 350°. In large bowl, cream butter with 1¼ cups sugar and ½ tablespoon cinnamon until light and fluffy. Beat in egg yolks, honey, vanilla, and lemon extract.

2) In a separate bowl, combine flour, baking powder, salt, and cream of tartar; gradually add to creamed mixture, and mix well.

3) In a shallow bowl, combine remaining sugar and cinnamon.

4) Roll a heaping tablespoon of dough into a golf-ball size ball, then roll into a 6-inch log. Coat in cinnamon-sugar, and loosely wind into a circular spiral. Bake 8–10 minutes or until lightly browned. Remove to wire racks, and cool completely.

5) **Pecan Praline Topping:** In a saucepan over medium heat, combine sugars and milk; bring to a boil. Stir in butter, pecans, and vanilla. Return to a boil, stirring constantly. Remove from heat; let cool 2–5 minutes. Should be liquid enough to "glaze" but thick enough to set. Spoon over cookies. (Place wax paper under rack to catch excess.) Garnish with sprinkles or glitter!

Frosted Sugar Cookie Bars

MAKES 15–24

COOKIE BARS:

2½ cups all-purpose flour

½ teaspoon baking powder

½ teaspoon salt

½ cup butter, softened

1 cup sugar

1 egg

1½ tablespoons sour cream

1 teaspoon vanilla extract

FROSTING:

½ cup butter, softened

4 cups powdered sugar

¼ cup half-and-half

1 teaspoon vanilla

Pinch of salt

Several drops of food coloring (optional)

1) **Cookie Bars:** Preheat oven to 375°. Grease 9x13-inch baking dish; set aside.

2) In medium bowl, combine flour, baking powder, and salt.

3) In separate bowl, cream together butter and sugar until light and fluffy, about 3 minutes. Add egg, and combine well. Add sour cream and vanilla, and mix until completely blended.

4) Slowly add flour mixture to creamed mixture, until well combined. Using your hands, gently press batter into baking dish. (Tip: Spray fingers lightly with nonstick cooking spray to help with the stickiness.)

5) Bake 17–20 minutes, or until edges are lightly golden. Set aside on a cooling rack to cool completely.

6) **Frosting:** In medium bowl, cream together butter, powdered sugar, and half-and-half until light and fluffy. Stir in vanilla and salt; mix well. Add food coloring until desired color is reached.

7) Using an offset spatula, frost cooled cookie bars. Cut into squares to serve.

Blackberry Bars

SERVES 10–12

1½ cups sugar, divided

1 teaspoon baking powder

3 cups all-purpose flour

¼ teaspoon salt

Zest and juice of 1 lemon

2 sticks cold unsalted butter, cubed

1 egg

4 teaspoons cornstarch

1½ cups fresh blackberries (can use frozen, thawed)

Whipped cream and mint for garnish (optional)

1) Preheat oven to 375°. Coat a 9x13-inch baking pan with nonstick cooking spray.

2) In a large bowl, whisk together 1 cup sugar, baking powder, flour, salt, and lemon zest. Using a pastry blender, incorporate cubed butter and egg until crumbly.

3) In another bowl, combine lemon juice, cornstarch, and remaining ½ cup sugar. Gently toss in blackberries.

4) Pat half of crust mixture into pan. Top with blackberry mixture, then crumble remaining crust mixture on top. Bake until top is golden brown, 35–40 minutes.

5) Let cool completely, then refrigerate at least 2 hours before serving. Cut into small bars, and garnish with whipped cream and mint, if desired.

Cherry Pie Cake Bars

MAKES 24–33

Bar recipes are the perfect addition to potlucks because of the ease of serving. These Cherry Pie Cake Bars are similar to biting into a piece of cherry pie. The batter, however, is similar to a cake.

3 cups all-purpose flour

½ teaspoon salt

1 cup butter, softened

2 cups sugar

4 eggs

1 teaspoon vanilla extract

¼ teaspoon almond extract

1 (21-ounce) can cherry pie filling

GLAZE:

1 cup powdered sugar

½ teaspoon vanilla extract

½ teaspoon almond extract

1 tablespoon milk

1) Preheat oven to 350°. Grease a 9x13-inch baking dish.

2) Whisk together flour and salt; set aside. In bowl of electric mixer, beat butter and sugar until light and fluffy. Beat in eggs, one at a time, then add extracts.

3) Reduce mixer speed to low, and add dry ingredients, a little at a time, until well combined. Reserve 1½ cups batter. Spread remaining batter evenly into prepared baking dish. Top with cherry pie filling, spreading evenly. Drop spoonfuls of reserved batter over the top.

4) Bake 30–35 minutes, or until lightly golden and a toothpick inserted in center comes out clean. Cool completely on wire rack.

5) **Glaze:** Whisk powdered sugar with extracts and enough milk to reach desired consistency. Pour into resealable bag and cut a small tip from one corner (or use piping bag). Drizzle over cooled bars. Chill in refrigerator a couple of hours, then cut into squares, and serve slightly chilled.

Grandma's Oatmeal Raisin Cookies

MAKES 4–5 DOZEN

½ cup shortening

2 eggs

1¼ cups sugar

⅓ cup brown sugar

1 teaspoon vanilla extract

1¾ cups all-purpose flour

1 teaspoon baking soda

1 teaspoon salt

1 teaspoon cinnamon

2 cups oatmeal

¾ cup raisins

1) Preheat oven to 375°. Beat shortening, eggs, sugar, brown sugar, and vanilla extract until well combined.

2) In a separate bowl, whisk together flour, baking soda, salt, cinnamon, and oats. Gradually add to sugar mixture, scraping bowl between additions. Fold in raisins.

3) Using a cookie scoop, drop onto ungreased cookie sheets approximately 2 inches apart. Bake 10–12 minutes until lightly browned.

Maple Pralines

MAKES 2–3 DOZEN

2 cups sugar

1 cup dark brown sugar

3 tablespoons white corn syrup

1 cup whipping cream

Pinch of salt

3 teaspoons maple flavoring

2 cups pecan halves

1) Combine sugars, corn syrup, whipping cream, and salt over medium-high heat until the mixture reaches soft-ball stage (235°) on a candy thermometer.

2) Remove from heat. Add maple flavoring and pecans. Beat until creamy. Drop from metal spoon onto wax paper.

Bananas Foster Pralines

MAKES 3 DOZEN

1 cup sugar

1 cup light brown sugar

½ cup plus 2 tablespoons heavy cream

4 tablespoons unsalted butter, cubed

1 teaspoon banana extract

1 teaspoon rum extract

1½ cups pecan halves

1) In heavy saucepan, combine sugar, brown sugar, and cream. Heat on medium or medium-high until mixture comes to a boil. Once mixture starts to boil, turn heat down to medium-low. Attach a candy thermometer to pan. Stir occasionally, scraping down sides of pan, and continue to cook until mixture reaches 240°.

2) Once mixture has reached soft-ball stage (235°–240°), remove pan from heat, and add butter. Stir in extracts, and fold in pecans.

3) Quickly spoon pralines onto parchment-lined baking sheets. Allow to fully set at room temperature.

Helpful Tips for Making Pralines:

Pralines aren't difficult but they do require your undivided attention.

• Have your baking sheets lined with parchment paper before you begin.

• Have all ingredients premeasured and ready.

• Use a pot larger than you think you'll need. You'll need the extra space for the syrup bubbles. A 4-quart pot works nicely.

• Spray the spoon you'll be using to drop the pralines lightly with cooking spray. Works like a charm!

Cakes

Set up a Cupcake Stand

Move over lemonade and adios cookies; the cupcake stand is heading to a town near you! With a bit of clever marketing, including chalkboard "Fresh Baked" signs, your homemade cupcakes are sure to get the neighbors cheering. Add a matching bunting using strips of fabric for a truly customized look…guaranteed to bring in a few extra tips!

Classic Yellow Cupcakes with Chocolate Buttercream

MAKES 24 CUPCAKES

2 cups all-purpose flour

2 teaspoons baking powder

½ teaspoon salt

2 sticks butter, softened

1½ cups sugar

4 eggs

2 teaspoons vanilla extract

¾ cup milk

CHOCOLATE BUTTERCREAM:

3 cups powdered sugar

⅓ cup butter, softened

2 teaspoons vanilla

3 ounces unsweetened baking chocolate, melted, cooled

3–4 tablespoons milk

1) Preheat oven to 350°. Prepare muffin tins by lining with cupcake liners. Set aside.

2) Sift together flour, baking powder, and salt; set aside.

3) Using an electric mixer, cream together butter and sugar until light and fluffy. Beat in eggs one at a time; stir in vanilla.

4) Alternate adding flour mixture with milk, mixing until just incorporated. Don't overmix.

5) Divide batter into prepared muffin tins, filling each ¾ full. Bake 15–20 minutes, or until a toothpick inserted into center comes out clean. Cool completely before frosting.

6) **Chocolate Buttercream:** In medium bowl, beat powdered sugar and butter with an electric mixer on low speed until well combined. Stir in vanilla and chocolate.

7) Gradually beat in milk, a tablespoon at a time, until smooth and spreadable. If frosting is too thick, add more milk; if too thin, add a small amount of powdered sugar.

Brown Butter Pecan Cake

SERVES 6–8

3 sticks unsalted butter, browned, cooled*

2¼ cups light brown sugar

4 eggs

2 teaspoons vanilla

3 cups cake flour

1 teaspoon salt

1 teaspoon baking powder

⅛ teaspoon baking soda

1 teaspoon cinnamon

½ teaspoon nutmeg

1 cup whole milk

⅔ cup sour cream

1 cup chopped pecans

BUTTERCREAM FROSTING:

2 sticks unsalted butter, browned, cooled*

5–6 cups powdered sugar

½ teaspoon cinnamon

¼ teaspoon nutmeg

1 teaspoon salt

4–5 tablespoons milk

1½ teaspoons vanilla

⅔ cup finely chopped pecans

1) Preheat oven to 350°. Spray bottom of 3 (8-inch) cake pans with nonstick baking spray, line with cut-to-fit parchment paper, and lightly spray parchment paper as well.

2) In bowl of stand mixer, beat butter and sugar 3–4 minutes until fluffy. Beat in eggs, one at a time, and add vanilla.

3) In a separate bowl, combine flour, salt, baking powder, baking soda, cinnamon, and nutmeg. Add to butter mixture in thirds, alternating with milk and sour cream. Mix well. Fold in pecans.

4) Pour batter into pans; bake 22–25 minutes, or until a toothpick inserted in center comes out clean. Cool on wire racks.

5) **Buttercream Frosting:** In bowl of a stand mixer, beat butter until smooth.

6) To mixer bowl, add powdered sugar, cinnamon, nutmeg, and salt; beat on low. Add milk and vanilla; increase speed, whipping until fluffy. Fold in pecans.

7) Frost between layers of cooled cake, then frost top and sides.

*Heat butter in saucepan over medium heat, stirring occasionally, until brown solids form. Transfer to bowl and refrigerate until solid; set out to cool to room temperature before using.

Layered "Naked" Carrot Cake

Layered "Naked" Carrot Cake

SERVES 6–8

Unlike some carrot cakes that may have icing both inside as well as covering their outer layers, this cake only has icing between the layers leaving it's outside "naked."

2 cups sugar

1½ cups vegetable oil

4 large eggs

2 cups all-purpose flour

2 teaspoons baking powder

1 teaspoon baking soda

1 teaspoon salt

1½ teaspoons ground cinnamon

¾ teaspoon ground nutmeg

½ cup seedless raisins

2½ cups finely grated peeled carrots

1 cup chopped walnuts

FROSTING:

4 cups powdered sugar

2 (8-ounce) packages cream cheese, softened

1 stick unsalted butter, softened

4 teaspoons vanilla extract

1) Preheat oven to 325°. Lightly spray 3 (9-inch) cake pans with nonstick cooking spray, then line bottom with cut-to-fit wax paper, and coat wax paper, too; set aside.

2) Using electric mixer, beat sugar and oil. Add eggs, 1 at a time, beating well after each addition.

3) In a separate bowl, combine flour, baking powder, baking soda, salt, cinnamon, and nutmeg. Gradually add to sugar mixture. Stir in raisins and grated carrots. Mix well.

4) Divide batter equally into prepared pans. Bake 40–45 minutes, or until toothpick inserted into center comes out clean, and cake begins to pull away from sides of pans. Cool in pans on racks 15 minutes. Turn out cakes onto racks, and cool completely.

5) **Frosting:** Using an electric mixer, beat all ingredients until smooth and creamy.

6) Using icing spatula, spread ⅓ of frosting on bottom cake layer. Top with another cake layer. Spread with ⅓ of frosting. Top with remaining cake layer. Spread remaining ⅓ of frosting on top of cake, then sprinkle with chopped walnuts.

Red Velvet White Chocolate Cake

SERVES 10

3½ cups cake flour

½ cup unsweetened cocoa powder

1½ teaspoons salt

2 cups canola oil

2¼ cups sugar

3 eggs

3 ounces red food coloring

1½ teaspoons vanilla

1¼ cups buttermilk

2 teaspoons baking soda

2½ teaspoons white vinegar

WHITE CHOCOLATE FROSTING:

2 (8-ounce) packages cream cheese, cold

1½ sticks butter, softened

1 tablespoon plus 1 teaspoon vanilla extract

8 ounces white chocolate, melted gently in microwave and cooled slightly

6 cups powdered sugar, sifted

1) Preheat oven to 350°. Grease 3 (9-inch) round cake pans with butter, and line the bottoms with parchment, cut to fit.

2) Whisk together flour, cocoa, and salt in a bowl.

3) Beat oil and sugar with an electric mixer on medium until well blended. Beat in eggs, one at a time. Lower mixer speed to low, and carefully add red food coloring. Add vanilla, then alternately add flour mixture and buttermilk, half at a time, ending with buttermilk. Scrape down sides of bowl, and mix to combine.

4) Combine baking soda and vinegar in a small dish. Add to batter with mixer running, beating just until combined.

5) Divide batter between the 3 cake pans. Bake 40–45 minutes or until a cake tester, or toothpick, inserted into center comes out clean. Cool 10–20 minutes, remove from pan, and peel off parchment. Cool completely on wire racks before icing.

6) **White Chocolate Frosting:** Beat cream cheese, butter and vanilla until blended. Mix in white chocolate. Add powdered sugar slowly (2 cups at a time), and beat until smooth.

Italian Crème Cake

SERVES 6–8

CAKE:

2 cups sugar

1 stick butter, softened

½ cup vegetable shortening

5 large eggs, separated

2 cups all-purpose flour

1 teaspoon baking soda

½ teaspoon salt

1 cup buttermilk

1 cup chopped pecans, toasted

1 cup shredded coconut

1 teaspoon vanilla extract

CREAM CHEESE FROSTING:

1 stick butter, softened

1 (8-ounce) package cream cheese, softened

1 teaspoon vanilla extract

1 (1-pound) package powdered sugar

½ cup chopped pecans

1) **Cake:** Preheat oven to 350°. Grease and flour 3 (9-inch) cake pans.

2) In a large mixing bowl, cream together sugar, butter, and shortening. Add egg yolks, one at a time, mixing well.

3) Sift together flour, baking soda, and salt. Add to creamed mixture in 3 batches, alternating with buttermilk, beginning and ending with flour. Mix well. Stir in pecans, coconut, and vanilla.

4) In a separate bowl, beat egg whites to stiff peaks with mixer. Gently fold into batter, and pour into prepared pans.

5) Bake about 25 minutes, or until layers start to pull away at the sides and a toothpick inserted in center comes out clean. Cool slightly in pan, then invert onto a wire rack to cool completely.

6) **Cream Cheese Frosting:** Beat together butter, cream cheese, vanilla, and sugar with a mixer until fluffy.

7) When cake has completely cooled, frost between layers, then frost top of cake. Sprinkle with pecans.

Strawberry Shortcakes with Sweet Cream Biscuits

SERVES 6–8

2 cups strawberries

¼ cup sugar

BALSAMIC REDUCTION:

2 tablespoons balsamic vinegar

2 tablespoons sugar

SWEET CREAM BISCUITS:

2 cups all-purpose flour

⅓ cup sugar

2½ teaspoons baking powder

½ teaspoon salt

1½ cups heavy cream

Whipped cream for garnish

1) Rinse strawberries, slice, and place in a bowl. Sprinkle with sugar, and stir to coat. Cover with plastic wrap, and chill 30 minutes or longer before serving. The strawberries will make their own syrup as they chill.

2) **Balsamic Reduction:** Bring vinegar and sugar to a simmer in a small saucepan. Cook until mixture reduces by half.

3) **Sweet Cream Biscuits:** Preheat oven to 450°. Mix flour, sugar, baking powder, and salt in a large bowl. Gradually stir in cream. Continue to mix with floured hands until well combined. Place on a lightly floured surface, and roll 1 inch thick. Cut with a 2- or 3-inch biscuit cutter. Place on ungreased baking sheet. Bake 10–12 minutes, or until light brown.

4) Assemble by placing 2 biscuits on each serving plate. Top with strawberries, and drizzle with Balsamic Reduction. Garnish with whipped cream.

Cinnamon Coffee Cake

SERVES 6

1 stick butter, softened

2 large eggs

1 cup sour cream

2 cups all-purpose flour

1 teaspoon baking soda

1 teaspoon baking powder

1½ teaspoons ground cinnamon

1 cup sugar

Vanilla bean seeds, scraped from 1 vanilla bean pod

½ cup chopped pecans

¼ cup whole milk

1) Preheat oven to 350°. Grease and flour a 9-inch square baking pan.

2) Mix together butter, eggs, and sour cream in a large bowl until well blended. Add flour, baking soda, baking powder, cinnamon, and sugar. Stir in vanilla seeds and pecans, then slowly stir in milk.

3) Pour batter into prepared pan, and bake 30–35 minutes, or until a toothpick inserted into center comes out clean. Remove from the oven, and cool slightly.

RECIPE IN A JAR VARIATION:

For a special take-home gift, layer this recipe in a Mason jar!

1) Mix together flour, baking soda, and ground cinnamon. Place in a 1-quart jar. Top with a layer of cinnamon chips.

2) Mix together sugar and vanilla bean seeds, and add as a layer in the jar. Top with chopped pecans, and seal. Decorate the lids, and include baking instructions.

Honey Bun Cake

Honey Bun Cake

SERVES 8–10

Whenever we go on a road trip, I insist on getting a convenience store honey bun. It drives my husband bonkers. "Aimee, do you know how bad those things are for you?" But I don't care. Honey buns and road trips go together like peas and carrots in my book. We just so happened to be joking about my honey bun road-tripping tendencies as we were traveling back from an antique shopping trip where I picked up several vintage cookbooks. Low and behold, there was a recipe for Honey Bun Cake! It needed a few tweaks, but by golly, it is fantastic. If I could figure out how to eat it in the car without a fork, I might eliminate my need for the packaged ones!

1 box yellow cake mix

1 box vanilla instant pudding mix

1 cup buttermilk

¾ cup vegetable oil

½ cup sugar

4 eggs

1 cup packed light brown sugar

3 teaspoons cinnamon

1 cup chopped pecans

ICING:

1 cup powdered sugar

1 teaspoon vanilla extract

3 tablespoons milk

1) Preheat oven to 350°. Grease 9x13-inch baking dish; set aside.

2) In bowl of stand mixer, mix together cake mix, pudding mix, buttermilk, oil, sugar, and eggs.

3) In separate bowl, mix together brown sugar, cinnamon, and chopped pecans. Fold into batter, and combine by hand.

4) Bake 30–35 minutes or until cake is golden brown and toothpick inserted in center comes out clean.

5) **Icing:** Combine all ingredients, and pour over cake while still warm.

Mississippi Mud Cake

SERVES 15–24

1 cup chopped pecans

2 sticks butter

1 (4-ounce) semisweet chocolate baking bar, chopped

2 cups sugar

1½ cups all-purpose flour

½ cup unsweetened cocoa

4 large eggs

1 teaspoon vanilla extract

1 teaspoon salt

1 (10½-ounce) bag miniature marshmallows

CHOCOLATE GLAZE:

1 stick butter

⅓ cup milk

¼ cup unsweetened cocoa

1 (16-ounce) package powdered sugar

1 teaspoon vanilla extract

1) Preheat oven to 350°. Place pecans in a single layer on an ungreased cookie sheet. Bake 8–10 minutes, until lightly toasted.

2) Microwave 2 sticks butter and chopped chocolate bar in a large microwave-safe glass bowl at HIGH power 1 minute, stirring halfway through. Whisk sugar, flour, cocoa, eggs, vanilla extract, and salt into chocolate mixture. Pour batter into a greased 10x15-inch jellyroll pan.

3) Bake at 350° for 20 minutes. Remove from oven, top evenly with marshmallows, and bake 8–10 minutes longer. Drizzle warm cake with Chocolate Glaze, and sprinkle with toasted pecans.

4) **Chocolate Glaze:** Melt butter in a saucepan over medium heat. Whisk in milk and cocoa, and bring to a boil, whisking constantly. Remove from heat.

5) Gradually add powdered sugar, stirring until smooth; stir in vanilla. If too thick, add 1 tablespoon milk, until desired consistency is reached. Use immediately.

Katie's Chocolate Chip Snack Cakes

SERVES 8–10

My friend and former co-worker, Katie Jones, sent me a handwritten copy of her mama's snack cake recipe. Katie remembers having it frequently as an afterschool treat when she was growing up. I made it for supper club one night, and it was all I had in me not to take credit for it when all the rave reviews were coming in! Thanks, Katie.

1¾ cups boiling water

1 cup uncooked oatmeal

1 cup lightly packed brown sugar

1 cup granulated sugar

2 sticks butter, softened

2 extra large or 3 small eggs

1¾ cups unsifted all-purpose flour

½ teaspoon salt

1 teaspoon baking soda

1 tablespoon cocoa

1 (12-ounce) package semisweet chocolate chips, divided

¾ cups chopped walnuts or pecans

1) Pour boiling water over oatmeal. Add brown sugar, granulated sugar, and butter; stir until butter is melted, and let stand at room temperature for 10 minutes.

2) Add eggs to oatmeal mixture, and mix well.

3) In a separate bowl, sift together flour, salt, baking soda, and cocoa, and add to oatmeal mixture. Combine well. Fold in half the chocolate chips.

4) Pour into well-greased and floured 9x13-inch baking pan. Sprinkle with remaining chocolate chips and nuts. Bake at 350° for 40 minutes, or until toothpick inserted in center comes out clean.

Pies

Cute Pie Cutout Decorations

Using cookie cutters is a creative way of embellishing your pie crusts. Use letters to create special messages, a leaf cutter for a unique autumn pie, a heart cutter for a special Valentine's Day pie, or a star cutter for a star-spangled apple pie, perfect for the 4th of July. Before baking, place the cutout directly on the pie (shown here) for a one-crust pie, or on top crust of a two-crust pie, or cut the shape from top crust and they will double as vents.

Grasshopper Pie with Thin Mint Cookie Crust

SERVES 6–8

PIE FILLING:

24 marshmallows

½ cup milk

¼ cup green crème de menthe

2 tablespoons crème de cacao

1 cup heavy cream

CRUST:

1 sleeve (about 16) Thin Mint cookies, crumbled, divided

1 chocolate wafer crust, crumbled

3 tablespoons butter, melted

1) **Pie Filling:** Melt marshmallows in milk over medium heat in a small saucepan; let cool. Add crème de menthe and crème de cacao.

2) In a chilled mixing bowl, whip cream until stiff peaks form; fold into cooled marshmallow mixture, and set aside.

3) **Crust:** Reserve ¼ cup cookie crumbs. In a large bowl, combine remaining cookie crumbs, crumbled wafer crust, and butter. Press into bottom and side of 9-inch pie pan.

4) Spoon Pie Filling into Crust, smooth with a spatula, and pop into freezer for about 2 hours.

5) Allow to thaw on countertop about 10 minutes prior to serving, then sprinkle edges with reserved ¼ cup cookie crumbs. Serve chilled.

Sinfully Southern Chocolate-Pecan Pie

SERVES 6–8

1 refrigerated pie crust

1½ cups pecan halves

4 ounces bittersweet chocolate, finely chopped

3 large eggs

¾ cup dark corn syrup

⅔ cup sugar

¼ cup firmly packed dark brown sugar

5 tablespoons unsalted butter, melted, slightly cooled

1 tablespoon all-purpose flour

1 tablespoon vanilla extract

½ teaspoon salt

1) Preheat oven to 350°.

2) Fit crust into a 9-inch pie plate, folding edges under, and crimping as desired. Sprinkle pecans and chocolate in bottom.

3) In a large bowl, whisk eggs until foamy. Add corn syrup, sugars, melted butter, flour, vanilla, and salt; whisk until thoroughly combined. Pour over pecans and chocolate.

4) Bake until crust is golden brown, and filling is set, 45–50 minutes. Loosely cover with foil during the last 10 minutes, or use a pie shield to avoid excessive browning. Let cool completely on a wire rack before slicing.

Sweet Potato S'Mores Pie

Sweet Potato S'Mores Pie

SERVES 6–8

1¼ cups graham cracker crumbs

4 tablespoons unsalted butter, melted

¾ cup plus 2 tablespoons sugar, divided

1½ teaspoons ground cinnamon, divided

1¼ teaspoons kosher salt, divided

2 (4-ounce) semisweet chocolate bars

2 cups cooked puréed sweet potato (2–3 sweet potatoes)

¾ cup condensed milk

3 large eggs, lightly beaten

½ teaspoon ground nutmeg

2 cups miniature marshmallows

1) Preheat oven to 350°. Coat (9-inch) pie plate with nonstick cooking spray.

2) In medium bowl, stir together graham cracker crumbs, melted butter, 2 tablespoons sugar, ½ teaspoon cinnamon, and ¼ teaspoon salt until combined. Firmly press into bottom of pie plate and slightly up side. Bake until light golden brown, about 12 minutes. Cool completely on a wire rack.

3) In a small microwave-safe bowl, heat chocolate in 30-second intervals until melted, stirring in between each interval. Spread chocolate evenly over cooled crust. Freeze until firm, 10–15 minutes.

4) In a medium bowl, combine sweet potato, remaining ¾ cup sugar, condensed milk, eggs, remaining 1 teaspoon cinnamon, remaining 1 teaspoon salt, and nutmeg until smooth. Pour over chocolate layer.

5) Bake until center is set, 45–50 minutes. Let cool completely on a wire rack, then refrigerate at least 3 hours. Sprinkle evenly with marshmallows.

6) Bake at 350° until marshmallows are lightly toasted, about 5 minutes.

Peach Crisp Pie

SERVES 6–8

1 refrigerated pie crust

¾ cup all-purpose flour

⅓ cup sugar

½ cup light brown sugar

6 tablespoons cold butter, cubed

4 cups peeled, sliced fresh peaches

2 tablespoons cinnamon-sugar mixture (¼ cup sugar plus 1 tablespoon cinnamon)

1) Preheat oven to 375°. Place pie crust into greased 9- or 10-inch pie dish.

2) In a small bowl, combine flour and sugars, and cut in butter until mixture resembles wet sand. Sprinkle half the mixture into crust, arrange peaches evenly in dish, then top with remaining crumb mixture. Sprinkle cinnamon-sugar over top.

3) Bake 35–40 minutes, or until filling is bubbly, and peaches are tender.

My-Oh-My Apple Pie

SERVES 6–8

½ cup sugar

½ cup light brown sugar

3 tablespoons all-purpose flour

1 teaspoon ground cinnamon

¼ teaspoon ground nutmeg

6 cups thinly sliced apples, peeled (about 5 apples)

1 tablespoon lemon juice

2 refrigerated pie crusts

2 tablespoons butter, melted

1 tablespoon vanilla extract

1 egg white

1 tablespoon sugar

1 teaspoon cinnamon

1) In a small bowl, combine sugars with flour and spices; set aside.

2) In a separate bowl, toss apples with lemon juice. Add to sugar mixture, and toss to coat.

3) Line a 9-inch pie pan with 1 crust, and fill with apple mixture. Whisk together melted butter and vanilla extract, and pour on top.

4) Roll out remaining pie crust; cut into strips about ¾ inch wide. Create a lattice effect on top of pie by weaving strips under and over each other. Trim edges.

5) Beat egg white until foamy; brush over top of pie. Combine sugar and cinnamon, and sprinkle on top. Use a pie shield to place over edges of pie (or aluminum foil) to keep edges from browning too quickly.

6) Bake at 375° for 25 minutes. Remove shield, and bake an additional 20–25 minutes, until crust is golden brown and filling is bubbly. Cool. Serve at room temperature.

Old-Fashioned Maple Syrup Pie

SERVES 6–8

BUTTER CRUST:

1¼ cups all-purpose flour

¼ teaspoon salt

1 stick cold butter, cut into small pieces

3–5 tablespoons ice water

FILLING:

2 eggs, beaten

1 cup maple syrup

2 tablespoons unsalted butter, melted

1 cup brown sugar

½ cup chopped pecans

2 tablespoons all-purpose flour

1) **Butter Crust:** In a medium bowl, combine flour and salt. Using a pastry blender, incorporate cold butter into flour mixture until size of tiny peas. Add ice water, a tablespoon at a time, and mix until dough forms a soft ball. Flatten dough into a disc, wrap in plastic, and let rest in refrigerator about an hour.

2) Preheat oven to 375°. Roll out chilled pie dough large enough to line a 9-inch pie plate. Press lightly into bottom and side of plate.

3) **Filiing:** Combine all ingredients until thoroughly combined. Spread evenly into crust.

4) Bake 45–50 minutes, or until Filling forms a crust, but pie is still somewhat gooey. Cool on a wire rack at least 1 hour prior to serving. Serve at room temperature; refrigerate remaining pie.

Tiramisù Pie

SERVES 6–8

CRUST:

1¾ cups crushed chocolate shortbread cookies

½ stick butter, melted

2 tablespoons sugar

FILLING:

1 (3.3-ounce) box white chocolate instant pudding mix

1½ cups heavy whipping cream

1½ (8-ounce) containers mascarpone cheese

¼ cup powdered sugar

TOPPING:

1½ cups heavy whipping cream

2 tablespoons cocoa powder

¾ cup powdered sugar

Grated semisweet chocolate, additional shortbread cookies for garnish (optional)

1) **Crust:** Preheat oven to 350°. In medium bowl, combine cookie crumbs, melted butter, and sugar. Press crumb mixture into bottom and up side of 9-inch deep-dish pie plate. Bake 8 minutes; set aside to cool.

2) **Filling:** In medium bowl, beat pudding mix and cream at medium speed with an electric mixer until soft peaks form. Add mascarpone, beating until well combined. Beat in powdered sugar. Spoon Filling into prepared Crust, and chill 1 hour.

3) **Topping:** In medium bowl, beat cream and cocoa powder at medium-high speed with electric mixer until soft peaks form. Add powdered sugar, and beat until stiff peaks form. Spread over Filling. Garnish with grated chocolate and a couple of cookies, if desired.

Strawberry Mousse Pretzel Pie

Strawberry Mousse Pretzel Pie

SERVES 6–8

Light and fluffy, cool and creamy, this pie is the epitome of summertime. The strawberry filling combined with pretzel crust, makes the perfect balance of sweet and salty. Even better? Minus the crust, it eliminates the need to bake. No need to keep the oven on longer than necessary once the temperatures start to soar. Topped with a heap of whipped cream and a sprig of mint, it's perfectly suited for a birthday treat on the porch.

CRUST:

2 cups finely crushed pretzel sticks

6 tablespoons butter, melted

¼ cup firmly packed light brown sugar

FILLING:

1 (14-ounce) can sweetened condensed milk

½ (8-ounce) package cream cheese, softened

4 tablespoons plus 1 teaspoon strawberry gelatin, or ½ (3-ounce) package

2 cups sliced fresh strawberries, puréed and strained, seeds discarded

2 cups whipping cream, divided

⅓ cup sugar

1) **Crust:** Preheat oven to 350°. Mix all ingredients; firmly press on bottom, up side, and onto lip of lightly greased 10-inch pie plate. Bake 10–12 minutes or until lightly browned. Remove from oven to a wire rack, and cool completely.

2) **Filling:** Beat condensed milk, cream cheese, and gelatin at medium speed with an electric mixer until smooth. Add strawberry purée, and beat at low speed just until blended. Transfer to a large bowl.

3) Beat ¾ cup whipping cream at high speed until soft peaks form; gently fold into strawberry mixture. Spoon into prepared Crust. Cover, and freeze 8–12 hours or until firm.

4) Beat remaining 1¼ cups whipping cream at high speed until foamy; gradually add sugar, beating until soft peaks form. Spread over pie.

5) Freeze 1 hour or until whipped cream is firm. Serve chilled.

Lemon Icebox Pie

SERVES 6–8

VANILLA WAFER CRUST:

2 cups vanilla wafer crumbs (about 4 cups vanilla wafers)

½ cup butter, melted

2 teaspoons sugar

⅛ teaspoon salt

FILLING:

1 (8-ounce) package cream cheese, softened

1 (14-ounce) can sweetened condensed milk

½ cup coconut milk

1 tablespoon lemon zest

⅓ cup fresh lemon juice

4 cups frozen whipped topping, thawed, divided

Lemon slices and fresh mint for garnish

1) **Vanilla Wafer Crust:** In a medium bowl, stir together wafer crumbs, melted butter, sugar, and salt. Press mixture into bottom and up side of 9-inch pie plate. Place in freezer while you make Filling.

2) **Filling:** In a large bowl, beat cream cheese at medium speed with a mixer until smooth. Add condensed milk, coconut milk, lemon zest, and lemon juice; beat until combined. Gently whisk in ½ cup whipped topping. Pour into crust. Place a piece of plastic wrap directly on surface of filling, and freeze until firm, about 4 hours.

3) Let stand 20 minutes at room temperature before serving. Uncover pie, top with remaining whipped topping, and garnish with lemon slices and mint.

Garnish Tip:

Cut your lemon slice into thirds to create flower petals. Attach a sprig of mint to the bottom and you have a dainty topping for your Lemon Icebox Pie that is a bit "out of the box."

Banana Pudding Pie

SERVES 6–8

1 (12-ounce) box vanilla
  wafers, divided

3 tablespoons butter, melted

2 large bananas, sliced

PUDDING FILLING:

¾ cup sugar

⅓ cup all-purpose flour

2 large eggs

4 egg yolks (save the whites!)

1¾ cups milk

3 tablespoons condensed milk

2 teaspoons vanilla extract

MERINGUE:

4 eggs whites

½ cup sugar

1) Preheat oven to 350°. Set aside 20–30 vanilla wafers; pulse remaining wafers in a food processor until coarsely crushed. Combine melted butter with crushed wafers until blended. Firmly press into bottom of 9-inch pie dish, and bake 10–12 minutes until lightly browned. Remove to a wire rack, and cool.

2) Arrange a layer of banana slices evenly over cooled crust.

3) **Pudding Filling:** Whisk together sugar, flour, eggs, egg yolks, and milks. Cook over medium-low heat, whisking constantly 8–10 minutes or until thick and can hold soft peaks. Remove from heat; stir in vanilla. Spread a third of pudding over bananas.

4) Top with half of reserved vanilla wafers. Spread more pudding over wafers, repeating with bananas and wafers and ending with pudding.

5) **Meringue:** Beat egg whites on high until foamy. Gradually add sugar until stiff peaks form. Spread over pie and bake at 250° for 10–12 minutes until golden brown.

6) Remove from oven and cool. Refrigerate and serve chilled.

Other Desserts

Washi Tape Flags

Blueberry Cheesecakes baked in Mason jars are perfect for individual portioning. Make them extra special by attaching Washi Tape flags in your theme's decor directly onto their serving utensils. Adds a pop of color and literally takes you moments to create.

Mason Jar Lemon Bars

SERVES 6

1 box yellow cake mix

2 eggs, divided

⅓ cup oil

1 (8-ounce) package cream cheese, softened

⅓ cup sugar

1 teaspoon lemon juice

Whipped cream (optional)

1) Preheat oven to 350°.

2) Mix dry cake mix, 1 egg, and oil until crumbly; reserve 1 cup, and set aside. Divide remaining mixture into 6 (4-ounce) ungreased Mason jars, and lightly pat in bottom. Place jars on a cookie sheet, and bake 15–18 minutes, or until lightly browned. Set aside to cool.

3) Beat cream cheese, sugar, lemon juice, and remaining egg until light and smooth. Spread over baked layer, sprinkle with reserved crumble mixture. Bake 15 minutes longer. Cool. Top with whipped cream and a sprig of mint.

Blueberry Pecan Cobbler

SERVES 6–8.

1½ sticks butter

1½ cups sugar, divided

¾ cup all-purpose flour

1½ teaspoons baking powder

1 teaspoon salt

¾ cup milk

1 tablespoon lemon juice

2 cups blueberries, rinsed and patted dry

1 cup chopped pecans

Whipped cream for garnish

1) Preheat oven to 350°. Melt butter in a 9x11-inch pan in preheating oven.

2) In a medium-size bowl, mix ¾ cup sugar, flour, baking powder, and salt. Stir in milk, blending well, and removing clumps.

3) In a separate bowl, add remaining ¾ cup sugar and lemon juice to blueberries.

4) Remove baking dish from oven, and place blueberry mixture on top of melted butter. Pour batter on top of blueberries, and sprinkle with chopped pecans. Do not stir.

5) Bake 30 minutes or until a toothpick inserted into center comes out clean. Top individual servings with a dollop of whipped cream, if desired.

Peach Variation:

Replace blueberry mixture with 4 cups peeled and sliced peaches. Combine peaches, 1 cup sugar, and ½ cup water in a saucepan on medium-high heat. Bring to a boil, and simmer 10 minutes. Remove from heat, and proceed as above, omitting pecans.

Dulce de Leche Brownies

Dulce de Leche Brownies

SERVES 8

DULCE DE LECHE SAUCE:

1 cup light brown sugar

1 cup heavy whipping cream

½ cup sweetened condensed milk

BROWNIES:

1 stick butter

1 cup semisweet chocolate chips

¼ cup unsweetened cocoa powder

1 teaspoon vanilla

1 cup sugar

½ teaspoon salt

1 cup all-purpose flour

3 eggs, beaten

1) **Dulce de Leche Sauce:** Add brown sugar and whipping cream to a small-medium saucepan, and stir over medium heat until sugar dissolves. Continue to cook 5 minutes, stirring throughout. Stir in sweetened condensed milk. Remove from heat, and set aside.

2) Preheat oven to 350°. Line 8x8-inch pan with foil or parchment paper, and spray with nonstick spray. Set aside.

3) **Brownies:** In a medium saucepan, melt butter over medium heat. Add chocolate chips, and stir chocolate until melted. Remove from heat; stir in cocoa powder and vanilla.

4) In a large bowl, whisk sugar, salt, and flour. Pour chocolate mixture into flour, and add eggs. Mix well. Spread batter evenly in prepared baking pan.

5) Drizzle ⅓ Dulce de Leche Sauce over brownie batter. Use a knife to swirl sauce into batter. Bake 30–35 minutes until brownies are set. Allow to cool before cutting into squares, and serving drizzled with remaining Dulce de Leche Sauce. (If sauce has cooled too much, reheat in the microwave for about 20 seconds.)

Praline Bread Pudding with Bourbon Sauce

SERVES 10–12

12 cups cubed French bread (two 12-ounce loaves)

1½ cups chopped pecans

1 stick butter, melted

1½ cups milk

1 cup heavy cream

¾ cup firmly packed dark brown sugar

½ cup sugar

½ cup caramel syrup

1 teaspoon vanilla extract

½ teaspoon rum extract

5 large eggs, lightly beaten

BOURBON SAUCE:

1 (14-ounce) can sweetened condensed milk

¼ cup bourbon

½ cup dark brown sugar

1 stick butter, cut into pieces

1 teaspoon vanilla extract

1) Preheat oven to 350°. Grease a 9x13-inch baking dish; set aside.

2) Place bread cubes in a large mixing bowl. Add pecans and butter; tossing gently.

3) In a large saucepan, combine milk, cream, sugars, caramel syrup, and extracts. Bring to a simmer over medium heat, stirring frequently until sugar dissolves.

4) Remove from heat. Slowly add eggs to hot milk mixture, whisking constantly until smooth. Pour over bread mixture, and let stand 10 minutes, then pour into prepared baking dish, and place in a larger roasting pan. Pour enough hot water into roasting pan to reach halfway up side of baking dish. Bake 45 minutes. Loosely cover with foil, and bake an additional 30 minutes, or until custard is set and bread is golden brown. Remove from oven and hot water bath. Let cool 30 minutes. Serve warm, drizzled with Bourbon Sauce.

5) **Bourbon Sauce:** In a medium saucepan, simmer condensed milk and bourbon over medium heat, whisking constantly. Add brown sugar, and cook 1–2 minutes, continuing to whisk until mixture thickens. Remove from heat, and gradually whisk in butter. Stir in vanilla.

Mason Jar Blueberry Cheesecakes

SERVES 12

CRUST:

1¼ cups graham cracker crumbs

2 tablespoons sugar

⅓ cup butter, melted

CHEESECAKE:

1½ (8-ounce) packages cream cheese, softened

⅓ cup sugar

2 tablespoons fresh lime juice

1 teaspoon vanilla extract

2 large eggs

¼ cup blueberry preserves

½ cup fresh blueberries

1) Crust: Preheat oven to 325°. Lightly coat bottoms of 12 (4-ounce) Mason jars with nonstick cooking spray; set aside.

2) Combine graham cracker crumbs and sugar in a medium-size bowl. Stir in melted butter until thoroughly combined. Press about 1½ tablespoons crumb mixture into bottom of each Mason jar, using the back of the spoon to firmly pack. Bake about 6 minutes, then cool on wire rack.

3) Cheesecake: Beat cream cheese, sugar, lime juice, and vanilla with electric mixer at medium speed. Add eggs, one at a time, beating until yellow begins to disappear. Fill each Mason jar to the bottom of jar ring. Return to oven for another 15–18 minutes, until the Cheesecake begins to set. Cover, and refrigerate overnight, or at least 4 hours.

4) When ready to serve, top each with 1 teaspoon preserves, and a couple of fresh blueberries.

Topping Tip:

Don't let the blueberries fool you. These cheesecakes can be topped with just about anything your heart desires—cherry pie filling for a holiday party, or crushed pineapple for a delicious summertime snack. Drizzle it with chocolate, caramel, and pecans for a seriously sweet treat.

Banana Pudding Trifle

Banana Pudding Trifle

SERVES 8–12

You tell me one time when you've been to a church potluck and haven't had a banana pudding make an appearance. You can't do it, can you? Banana pudding might as well be synonymous with the word get-together—you really can't have one without the other. I've had a lot of banana pudding in my lifetime, and this one is the best! Rich, creamy, pull-on-your-stretchy-pants good!

PUDDING:

1 cup sugar

¼ cup cornstarch

Pinch of salt

4 large egg yolks

2 (12-ounce) cans evaporated milk

1 cup whole milk

4 teaspoons vanilla extract

TRIFLE:

2 cups heavy cream

2 teaspoons vanilla extract

1 (12-ounce) box vanilla wafers

6 bananas, peeled, sliced, plus more for garnish

Banana slices for garnish (drizzle with lemon juice to prevent browning)

1) **Pudding:** Whisk sugar, cornstarch, and salt in a small pot. Whisk in egg yolks; turn heat to medium, then vigorously whisk in evaporated milk and whole milk. Continue to whisk as it heats, until mixture boils and thickens to pudding consistency.

2) Remove from heat, and stir in 4 teaspoons vanilla extract. Transfer to bowl, and cover with plastic wrap directly on the surface to prevent a skin from forming; cool.

3) **Trifle:** When ready to assemble, whip cream with 2 teaspoons vanilla extract until soft peaks form.

4) Reserving 12 vanilla wafers, arrange 2 layers in a trifle dish in the following order: vanilla wafers, bananas, pudding, whipped cream.

5) Decorate top of trifle with reserved wafers along edges, or crumble wafers over top. Cover; refrigerate 2 hours until cookies soften, up to overnight. To serve, garnish with additional banana slices that have been drizzled with lemon juice.

Apple Crisp Pizza

SERVES 8

½ refrigerated or homemade pie crust

⅔ cup sugar

3 tablespoons all-purpose flour

1½ teaspoons ground cinnamon

4 medium apples (I like Gala), peeled and diced

TOPPING:

½ cup all-purpose flour

⅓ cup packed brown sugar

½ cup old-fashioned oats

1 teaspoon ground cinnamon

½ stick butter, softened

DRIZZLE:

½ cup caramel topping

1) Preheat oven to 350°.

2) Roll crust to fit a 12-inch pizza pan; fold edges under to give pizza a bit of a raised crust.

3) Combine sugar, flour, and cinnamon in a medium bowl. Add peeled, diced apples, and toss. Arrange apples in a single layer over crust to completely cover it.

4) **Topping:** Combine flour, brown sugar, oats, cinnamon, and butter in a bowl. Mix well. Sprinkle Topping evenly over apples. Bake 35–40 minutes or until apples are tender.

5) **Drizzle:** Remove from oven, and immediately drizzle with caramel topping. Cut into slices, and serve warm with ice cream.

Maple Pecan Popcorn

SERVES 8–10

8 cups plain popped popcorn

1 cup pecan pieces, toasted

6 tablespoons unsalted butter

1½ cups pure maple syrup

½ teaspoon salt

½ teaspoon maple extract

½ teaspoon cinnamon

1) Line a rimmed baking sheet with parchment paper. Lightly oil a rubber spatula to combine popcorn and pecans in a large bowl.

2) Melt butter in a heavy saucepan over medium-high heat; add maple syrup. Clip a candy thermometer to side of pan. Add salt, and bring to a boil. Reduce heat to medium to maintain a gentle boil, and cook without stirring until temperature reaches 290°, about 20 minutes. Watch carefully to avoid scorching.

3) Stir in maple extract and cinnamon, then pour over popcorn, stirring with spatula to help coat. Season with additional salt, if desired. Spread on lined baking sheet, allowing to cool completely before breaking into bite-size pieces. Store in airtight container.

Index

INDEX

INDEX

About the Author

**Crafter. Baker. Apron Maker.
Award-Winning Cookie Creator.**

After graduating from Louisiana College, then working in corporate insurance, Aimee Broussard traded in her successful career for the aprons and ovens, creations and comforts of her kitchen.

Armed with a recipe box full of family favorites, a Kitchen-Aid mixer received as a wedding gift, and a shiny new sewing machine, she set out to master the art of crafting, baking, and apron making. Some days she bakes, some days she crafts, but everyday she creates.

Aimee is the 2013 Dixie Crystals Cookie Bake-Off champion, bringing national recognition to her Pecan Praline King Cake Cookies. In 2014, she co-hosted several *Taste of Home Cooking School Live* shows spanning Louisiana, Alabama, and Mississippi, while showcasing her Honey Garlic Meatballs. Later that same year, she made her publishing debut with *The Traveling Apron Cookbook*, celebrating the friendships created from a spontaneous idea to circulate a handmade apron across the country while swapping recipes with strangers…strangers who would become friends, and friends who would become family.

A network blogger for both *Taste of Home* and AOL's Lifestyle Creative, Aimee's work has been featured in countless publications, both in print and online, including *Taste of Home Magazine, Taste of Home's Canning & Preserving, Woman's World, Country Living*, Today.com, Style Me Pretty and many others. This Fall you can virtually bring Aimee into your home with a series of baking videos produced with the Taste of Home Online Cooking School.

Southern born and raised, Aimee makes her home in Baton Rouge, Louisiana, with husband Brian and three ridiculously spoiled Cavalier King Charles Spaniels.